DON'T FORGET YOUR FREE BOOKS

GET THEM FOR FREE ON WWW.TRIVIABILL.COM

CONTENTS

INTRODUCTION

Welcome to *The Big Fat Book of Juicy Trivia*! In this book, you'll be introduced to a whole slew of fascinating facts from five different themes. This book is quite flexible and can be read from cover to cover or you can read a single chapter or even a separate story from a chapter at a time. You see, this book is divided into five specifically themed chapters and within each chapter; there are 15 to 20 stories full of amazing facts. At the end of each story are 20 or more random facts that will help you keep your trivia skills sharp.

This book will bring you to some pretty amazing places in the world, including some of the greatest national parks and will additionally introduce you to some geography that you probably have never considered.

You'll read about different types and elements of pop culture from around the world. From Hollywood to Bollywood and from K-Pop to Top 40, the modern world's obsession with film, fashion, television, and movies will be explored in an entertaining way which will keep you on track with the modern trends.

The wide world of sports is profiled in this trivia book as well. You will learn about the background of the world's most popular sports and a few things about some sports that are no longer played. This chapter also covers some elements of drinking and leisure culture, so have your drink recipe cards ready!

Finally, you'll read about some of the most fascinating—and some would say craziest—historically-based trivia stories. Some of these stories include the German emperor who died because he wore too much armor, the background of duels to the death, and some pretty interesting early examples of early medicine.

As flexible as this book is, it is also quite useful. You can use this book to study for trivia tournaments at your favorite pub, or you could use it for compiling questions if you are the DJ conducting the contests. This book is also perfect for a night with your friends and family when you're all sitting around the kitchen table thinking of something to do. It's certainly an icebreaker and conversation starter.

So, keep reading and be prepared for hours of non-stop entertainment.

CHAPTER 1:

Wild and Wonderful Places

FINDING GOD IN THE WORLD

Chances are, wherever you currently live, you don't have to travel far to find a spiritual location. It may just be a church or a wooded area where you feel at peace with the world, or it could be a larger, more well-known location. Most believers will tell you that God, or the Gods, can be found nearly everywhere, but there are just some places that seem to bring out the spirituality in all of us.

Perhaps the most spiritual of all cities is Jerusalem, Israel. The location of Jerusalem served as the location for various settlements throughout the Bronze Age, but it was when King David and the Israelites used the location as their capital city in the 11th century BCE that it became a spiritual city as we know it today.

King Solomon built the first temple in Jerusalem. Although it was destroyed, rebuilt, and then destroyed again, the foundation walls remain and are spiritually important for Jews. Jerusalem is also spiritually important for Christians, as the location of Jesus's final sermons and death. Muslims also view the city as an important site in their religion.

For more than one billion Roman Catholics in the world, the Vatican City is the most important site. Located entirely within Rome, the Vatican City is an independent nation-state that serves as the capital for Roman Catholicism and the home of the Pope. St. Peter's Basilica and the Sistine Chapel give the city a sense of awe and beauty, filling the hearts of all believers with the sense that they are in the presence of God.

In the middle of the desert in Saudi Arabia, you'll find the holiest site to the world's nearly two billion Muslims—Mecca (*Makkah al-Mukarramah - commonly shortened to Makkah)*. Mecca is both the birthplace of Islam's founder, Muhammad and the location of Kaaba Stone. More than three million devout Muslims make the trip to Mecca every year to fulfill the religious requirement—or "pillar"—of visiting the holy site at least once in their lives.

In India, you can visit the Ganges River, which is sacred to Hindus, and check out the Bodh Gaya, which is the place where Buddhists believe Buddha received his enlightenment under what became known as the Bodh Tree.

Random Facts:

- The annual pilgrimage—or *Hajj*—to Mecca takes place during the final month of the Islamic calendar.
- Ayers Rock, now known by its indigenous name, Uluru, is a spiritual location for the Aboriginal people in Australia. It is a monolithic sandstone rock formation that towers 1,142 feet above the flat countryside around it.
- The Painted Desert of the American southwest covers more than 93,500 acres of land and is located in two national parks: Grand Canyon National Park and the Petrified Forest National Park.
- Mount Fuji is a snowcapped volcano in Japan that stands 12,389 feet above the forest. It last erupted in 1708.
- The "Wailing Wall" or Western Wall is perhaps the holiest site in the religion of Judaism and is located in Jerusalem City. The limestone walls are all that remains of the Second Temple that was begun in 516 BCE and destroyed by the Romans in 70 CE. Religious observant Jews, as well as many non-Jews, who visit Israel make it a point to undertake a pilgrimage and pray at the Western Wall.
- Archaeologists believe that the spiritual site of Machu Picchu in Peru was built during the reign of the Inca King Pachacuti (1438-1471).
- The centerpiece of Bodh Gaya is the Bodhi Tree, which according to Buddhist tradition is where Buddha received his enlightenment. The Bodhi Tree has been destroyed numerous times throughout history but has miraculously grown back each time.
- The Shinto goddess Konohanasakuya-hime is the patroness of Mount Fuji.

- The residence of the Pope in Vatican City is known as the Apostolic Palace. In terms of the history of the Catholic Church, the Palace is relatively new, having been primarily built in the 16th century. The famous Sistine Chapel is within the Apostolic Palace.
- The Christ the Redeemer statue (Cristo Redenter) in Rio de Janeiro, Brazil, stands 98 feet tall and has an incredible 92-foot wingspan! The statue has been so spiritually inspiring that it has spawned many similar statues throughout the world, including the 66-foot tall Christ of the Ozarks in Arkansas.
- If you travel to the Sinai Peninsula in Egypt, you can visit Mount Sinai, the place where Moses received the Ten Commandments. Although not all people believe that the mountain that currently has the name is the actual Mount Sinai, those who ascend its 7,497 feet generally claim to have a spiritual experience.
- The Hagia Sophia in Istanbul, Turkey is one of the most spiritual locations in Europe. Most of the cathedral was built as a Greek Orthodox church in the 6th century CE by the Byzantine Emperor Justinian I (ruled 527-565). When the Ottoman Turks conquered the Byzantine Empire and renamed Constantinople Istanbul in 1453 it became and has continued to be a mosque.
- Non-Muslims are prohibited from entering the city of Mecca.
- Jerusalem during the time of Jesus was a thriving, cosmopolitan city thanks to the efforts of Herod the Great (ruled 37-4 BCE), who rebuilt much of the city.
- Hindus believe that the Ganges River is the earthly personification of the goddess Ganga. They believe that bathing in the river will cleanse them of their sins.
- The city of Kamakura, Japan is another notable spiritual location in Japan. It is known for its many Zen Buddhist and Shinto temples. A bronze 43-foot Buddha statue originally built in the 13th century is the focal point of the city.

- Christians believe the holiest site in Jerusalem—and their religion—is the Church of the Holy Sepulcher. They believe that the church was built on the site where Jesus was crucified and buried and then later ascended into Heaven.
- Although most people consider Confucianism a philosophy and not a religion, temples dedicated to the veneration—and some would say worship—of Confucius (551–479 BCE), can be found throughout China and other East Asian countries.
- The Romans destroyed the Second Temple in Jerusalem in retaliation against the Zealot Revolt (66-74 CE). The Zealots made their last stand on the mountain of Masada, which later became a sacred location to many of the Jewish faith.
- The Ganges River flows for more than 1,600 miles, originating in the Himalaya Mountains and terminating in the Bay of Bengal.

MANY, MANY NATIONS

There are seven continents on the Earth, but Antarctica is not considered a country or independent country or sovereign state, while Australia is both a sovereign state and a continent, which means that the 206 sovereign states of the planet are all concentrated on the remaining five continents.

What are some of these countries and how/why are there so many? And what exactly is a "sovereign state"? Is it any different from a nation-state, a republic, or a country?

A sovereign state is a country that is independent and autonomous. For instance, the United Kingdom is a sovereign state, while Northern Ireland is a country within that sovereign state and Bermuda is an overseas territory of the sovereign state. The same is true with the United States (sovereign state) and the U.S. Virgin Islands (territory).

Nation-states are essentially the same politically as sovereign states, although the term "nation" implies that all, or the majority, of the population shares the same language and/or culture.

A republic simply refers to the type of government employed by most sovereign states. Governments, in which a certain segment of the citizenry elect people to represent them in a congress or parliament; are considered republics. Even many dictatorships claim to be republics—the Democratic Republic of Korea (North Korea)—so the term is not always truly reflective of a country's status or even the style of government.

Finally, the term "country" is perhaps the most ambiguous of all these terms. All sovereign states, nation-states, and republics are countries, but many territories, colonies, and commonwealths can also be considered countries. Puerto Rico is a Commonwealth of the United States and therefore not a sovereign state, but many of its inhabitants, and even those descended from native-born Puerto Ricans, consider it to be a country unto itself.

Random Facts:

- The tiny nation of San Marino is the oldest continual sovereign state in Europe. It was found in 301 CE when it broke away from the Roman Empire and established its current constitution in 1503-1504 CE.
- There are arguments over whether Japan or China is the oldest sovereign state in Asia. The Shang Dynasty formed in China in 1,766 BCE, but most of what is considered China wasn't unified until the Qin Dynasty won the "Period of Contending States" in 221 BCE. The Japanese consider the date of the birth of their nation to be 660 BCE, but the country devolved into warring fiefdoms and wasn't unified again until 1600 CE.
- The United States is the oldest sovereign state in the Americas, declaring its independence from Britain in 1776.
- Ethiopia and Liberia are the only two sub-Saharan sovereign states to never have been colonized by European sovereign states.
- Taiwan, which officially calls itself the Republic of China, lost its seat in the UN to the People's Republic of China (Mainland China) in 1971. Mainland China doesn't recognize Taiwan's sovereignty and considers it a breakaway state.
- "Microstate" is the term for a very small sovereign state, such as Vatican City or San Marino.
- Ecuador is the oldest sovereign state in South America, declaring its independence from Spain in 1830.
- Haiti is the second-oldest sovereign state in North America and the oldest in the Caribbean, declaring its independence from France in 1804.
- Egypt is arguably the oldest continuous sovereign state in Africa, and the world, having first formed around 3,100 BCE. Egypt,

though, was ruled by several foreign dynasties throughout late antiquity into the modern period. Ethiopia has been an independent (sovereign) state since 900 CE, giving it the official title as longest-running sovereign state in Africa.

- Hong Kong has never been a sovereign state. The city was a British colony from 1842 to 1997 and is now a semi-autonomous region within China.
- In 2011, South Sudan became the newest sovereign state recognized by the United Nations.
- The State of Palestine was declared in 1988 and has since been recognized by 138 other sovereign states. The United Nations lists Palestine as an observer state, but most notably, Israel refuses to recognize Palestine as a sovereign state.
- The smallest sovereign state in the world in physical size is Vatican City at less than 0.2 square miles. (Encircled by a 2-mile border with Italy, Vatican City is an independent city-state that covers just over 100 acres, making it one-eighth the size of New York's Central Park)
- The Vatican City is also the least populated of all sovereign states with only 825 citizens.
- Most African sovereign states didn't gain their sovereignty until the British and French empires dissolved after World War II.
- Samoa is a South Pacific country that has been a sovereign state since 1889. American Samoa is an unincorporated territory of the U.S. Although geographically and culturally close, the International Date Line separates the two countries, with American Samoa being just east of it.
- Russia is the largest sovereign state in the world in physical size, at more than six million square miles.
- Singapore is the most populous microstate, with more than five

million citizens. Since it comprises a single city occupying about 276 square miles, it is also one of the most densely-populated countries in the world.

- Montenegro became the newest European sovereign state when it broke from Serbia in 2006.
- Southern Ireland began its journey toward sovereign status when it became the Irish Free State from 1922 to 1937 (which is four fifths of Ireland). It later became the Irish Republic in 1948.

IT'S A JUNGLE OUT THERE

Our planet is covered in trees! To be more specific, there are about three trillion trees currently on Earth—yes, that's trillion with a "T"—which comes to about 420 trees per person! Approximately 30% of the Earth's surface is covered with forests, with every continent, except Antarctica, having plenty of forests and jungles, with some regions having more than others.

If Russia is included, Europe accounts for the most forest cover, at about one-quarter of the total forested area, but South America has the greatest density/per capita forested surface of any continent, because approximately half of South America is covered in trees.

Brazil and some of its neighboring countries are home to perhaps the most famous forest in the world, the Amazon Rain Forest, but there are thousands of forests around the globe. Forests near the North Pole are known as boreal forests. These forests primarily comprise hearty pine trees that can survive long winters. The forests nearest the equator are tropical forests, or jungles, of which rainforests are one specific type. A tropical rainforest is a tropical forest that has no dry season.

Temperate forests can be found distributed over the widest area in the world, although they are second to boreal forests in total landmass covered. Temperate forests tend to be quite diverse, having both deciduous and coniferous trees, with varying degrees of rainfall. There are temperate rainforests located throughout the world, from the Pacific Northwest to southern Japan and from Chile to New Zealand.

Forests are vital for the continued existence of our planet. They provide habitat for hundreds of animal species in the form of intricate ecosystems and the trillions of trees provide vital oxygen which is needed to sustain life here on Earth.

Earth's many forests and jungles are also a source of livelihood and entertainment for people. The lumber industry provides millions of people around the world with jobs and the lumber harvested is used to build new homes, to provide heat, and to create chairs, tables, and anything else made from wood.

Random Facts:

- More than half of the world's forests are within the borders of only five countries: Russia, China, the United States, Brazil, and Canada.
- "Jungle" is a non-scientific term that generally refers to tropical rainforests. It was largely replaced in the 1970s in favor of the more specific "tropical rainforest."
- Vatican City, Monaco, and Nauru are the only sovereign states which do not have a forest.
- Exactly what defines a forest is open to debate. Generally speaking, a forest is defined as an area with a high density of trees, an area of ground that is under a tree canopy, and by the amount of land covered by trees. A wooded area that doesn't meet those criteria is generally considered to be a Woodland.
- Forests can be further divided into five classes: primary, modified natural, semi-natural, protective forest plantation, and productive forest plantation.
- Forest ecosystems are arranged in four natural layers. First there are the primary consumers that eat the plants, then there are the secondary and tertiary consumers that feed on the consumers below them, and finally there are the forest decomposers, which return nutrients from dead plants and animals back into the ground.
- The vegetation of a forest is also divided into distinct layers. The forest floor consists of leaves and other biomaterials that are composting. The understory is the shrubs and bushes, while the canopy is the large trees that cover the entire forest. Tropical rainforests also have an emergent layer of trees that rise above the canopy.
- The boreal forests are also known by the Russian word "taiga."

- Although we cut down about 15 billion trees annually, at the current rate, it would take about 200 years to cut down every tree on the planet.
- The word *jungle* originates from the Sanskrit word *juṅgala* (meaning rough and arid. It came into the English language via Hindi in the 18th century. How that word came to define tropical forests is unknown.
- You may think of Australia as a country entirely comprised of beaches, deserts, and cities, but it has a diverse range of forests that cover about 19% of the country/continent's land area.
- Although bamboo is often considered a plant more specifically than a tree, bamboo forests cover about 250,000 square miles of land. Bamboo can grow up to 40 feet in height, which is more than enough to provide a canopy, fulfilling part of the proper definition of a forest.
- Forest plantations account for about 4% of the world's forests. Forests cover some 3.9 billion hectares (or 9.6 billion acres) which is approximately 30% of the world's land..
- Deforestation has become a major issue in recent years. Farmers in some poor countries clear-cut forestland to make room for planting crops. It is estimated that around 10% of the world's forests have been lost since 1990.
- Although Brazil is best known for its Amazon Rainforest, it is also home to the quite large Atlantic Forest, which covers nearly 300,000 acres of land and has several sub-forests, including "tropical moist forests." Very little of the Atlantic Forest remains and what does is highly fragmented.
- The forests continue to be vulnerable to logging and agricultural expansion, particularly soy production. Habitat loss and hunting put many species in danger of extinction.

- A laurel forest is one in a region with high humidity but mild temperatures. Laurel forests can be found in pockets throughout the southeastern United States (such as Laurel, Mississippi).
- Mangrove forests can be found in the coastal areas of every continent except Europe and Antarctica. Mangroves are small trees that grow in salt or brackish water.
- More than half of all plant and animal species on Earth live in rainforests.
- About 36% of the Earth's forests are considered "primary forests," which means a forest of native trees with little to no human interference. Brazil has the largest expanse of primary forests in the world.
- Semi-natural forests are forests that comprise a combination of native trees and planted trees.
- Although the areas of semi-natural and planted forests have increased, the area covered by primary forests decreases every year. Brazil and Indonesia have experienced the greatest loss in primary forests due to logging and de-forestation.

THE BIG BOYS ON THE BLOCK

Of all the more than 206 sovereign states and territories, the largest ones stand out. When it comes to countries, size does matter! The United States, China, Japan, Germany, and India have the highest gross domestic product (GDP) and they also happen to be among some of the largest countries in size and population.

The United States is the largest country in population on the North American continent and is second-largest in land area on the continent after Canada. The U.S. is also the third-most populous country in the world, with about 330 million people.

China has the most people of any country with about 1.5 billion, but not far behind is India with 1.3 billion people.

Japan may not seem like a very large country, but it is 11th in total population with about 126 million inhabitants, although it only comes in at 62nd in size. With that said, Japan is the largest island country in Northeast Asia and the second-largest island country in all of Asia after Indonesia. Japan is also the fourth-largest island country in the world—we'll get to island nations in another chapter of this book.

You may be thinking that Germany is the anomaly among the countries with the highest GDP tending to coincide with large size, right? Well, Germany is only 7th in total land area among European countries, but it is 2nd in population, with just over 83 million people. Only Russia is ahead of Germany in population at 146 million people, but that isn't exactly fair because much of Russia is actually in Asia.

Russia is 9th in overall population among all nations with over 146 million people and 1st in total land area with over 6.6 million square miles. Since Russia straddles both Europe and Asia, it is therefore the largest country on both of those continents and encompasses nearly 11% of the Earth's surface!

Random Facts:

- Kazakhstan is the largest landlocked country in the world and is the largest country in Central Asia with a land area of over one million square miles.
- Cuba is the largest Caribbean nation by both population and total land area. It has a population of 11,252,999 and a total land area of 42,426 square miles.
- Nigeria is the most populous African country with more than 198 million inhabitants, but Algeria has the most landmass of any African nation with 919,600 square miles. Algeria is also the largest country that is on the Mediterranean Sea and the largest Arab-speaking country.
- In addition to being the largest and most populous country in South America, Brazil is also the largest and most populous Portuguese-speaking country.
- Mexico is by far the largest country in both land area and population in Central America. It is also the most populous predominantly Spanish-speaking country with more than 129million people.
- Indonesia is 2nd in total land area of 741,100 sq. miles with a population of 266 million among Asian countries and is first in those categories among Southeast Asian nations.
- Indonesia is the fourth-largest Asian country, after China, India, and Saudi Arabia.
- Ukraine is the largest European nation that is entirely within the continent at 233,000 square miles. Ukraine is the second-largest of Europe's 43 countries. The only country larger than Ukraine is Russia.
- The current population of Egypt is 102 million and Egypt is the largest predominantly Arabic-speaking country.

- It may be hard to believe, but Russia has more total land area than Antarctica. The South Pole continent covers 5.5 million square miles; which is approximately 1.1 million less than Russia's land area at 6.6 million square miles.
- Mexico may be the most populous Spanish-speaking country, but Argentina is the largest in total land area with 1,073,500 square miles.
- Greenland is the world's largest territory/dependency (it is a territory of Denmark) in landmass, but Hong Kong is the largest territory/dependency in population with more than 7.5 million people.
- Sudan was once the largest country in Africa in total landmass, but after South Sudan became an independent nation, it dropped to 3rd on the list.
- Australia is both the most populous and largest country in Oceania (the South Pacific). Papua New Guinea is second in Oceania in both of those categories.
- You probably know that the United States is the second largest English-speaking country after India in land population, but do you know which is third? Pakistan! Nigeria is number four in population.
- Canada may be the largest country in North America in land area and 2nd in the world overall, but it's 3rd in the continent in population and 38th in the world with 38 million people.
- China and India combine to account for more than 36% of the world's population.
- If the European Union were counted as a single country it would rank 7th in total landmass and would be number three in population with 447 million people.
- There is debate over what is the largest French-speaking country in

the world. You may think that it is France, but the Democratic Republic of Congo is larger than France in land area and population. However, a large percentage of Congo's population of 89.5 million does not speak French, whereas most of France's 67,067,000 people speak French as a primary or secondary language.

- Although Kazakhstan is officially the largest landlocked nation in total landmass, Mongolia is the largest landlocked country with no sea access. Kazakhstan borders the inland Caspian Sea.
- Despite less than 18.2% of its population professing to be Buddhists, China still has the largest practicing Buddhist population in the world with more than 244 million followers. The total accounts for more than 50.1% of the world's Buddhist population.
- Indonesia has the most practicing Muslims in the world at 87.2% of the population with a total population of approximately 273.7 million people.

ISLANDS UNTO THEMSELVES

An island is simply a land area that is surrounded by water. The size of the island doesn't matter and neither does where it's located: islands can be found in lakes and rivers as well as seas and oceans. Since the majority of the Earth is covered in water, islands are pretty common and most nation-states that have coastlines—which is the vast majority of countries—have islands within their borders.

But some islands are countries unto themselves.

Geographically speaking, island nations can be divided into four categories: one main island, two primary islands, an archipelago, or a nation that shares an island with another nation.

The best example of one main island would be Australia, although the state of Tasmania is a separate island off its southern shore. An island nation with two primary islands would be New Zealand. Archipelago nations, which are a series of islands, are quite common and include Japan and the Bahamas. Haiti and the Dominican Republic are good examples of nations that share an island, as they share the same island, Hispaniola.

In ancient times, islands provided defense against invading armies so therefore, they were a desirable place to build kingdoms. The island of Crete, which is now part of Greece, was the site of the earliest European state, known as the Minoan culture. The Minoan culture was successful and long-lived, lasting from about 2,700 to 1,450 BCE, thanks in large part to its large navy, which could protect the island from outsiders.

Britain and Japan are the island nations with the longest continuous governments, having successfully developed mainly because they were able to defend their islands from the outsiders.

The defensive benefits of islands have largely diminished in the modern era, although today island nations often profit from tourism, shipping, oil extraction, and commercial fishing.

Random Facts:

- After Australia, Indonesia—which is an archipelago—is the largest island nation in total landmass and largest in population.
- The Åland Islands territory is an archipelago off the southwest Finnish coast. Although the islands are part of Finland's territory, they are considered autonomous and have been controlled by Sweden and Russia as well as Finland throughout history.
- The sovereign state of Cyprus is an island unto itself technically, although the breakaway state of Northern Cyprus is also on the island. Northern Cyprus is primarily Turkish ethnicity and is only recognized by Turkey.
- Although most Caribbean Islands are quite small and they are all claimed by one nation-state or another, only 2% of their landmass is inhabited.
- Madagascar, with a landmass of 224,533 square miles, is the third-largest island nation in the world and the largest in Africa. Madagascar is quite different than the rest of Africa, though, because the largest ethnic group in the country is Austronesian in origin originally from the Indonesian area.
- Malta is a two-island nation-state in the Mediterranean Sea with a long history. The islands were colonized by Phoenicians in ancient times, became part of the Carthaginian Empire in the 5th century BCE, and then the island was occupied by the Romans in the 3rd century BCE.
- Iceland is the most sparsely populated European sovereign state, with only 341,357 inhabitants on an island of 40,000 square miles.
- Indonesia claims more islands than any other island nation with 14,752.
- About 70 miles off the shore of Adelaide South Australia is a

curious place known as Kangaroo Island. More than 140,000 people visit the island every year to see kangaroos in the wild, but penguins are an even bigger attraction for many.

- During the Late Bronze Age (c. 1,500-1,200 BCE), the island of Cyprus was the location of a powerful kingdom known as Alashiya.
- Singapore is an island nation that is also a city-state.
- The Republic of Seychelles is an archipelago nation in the Indian Ocean that is considered part of the African continent. It has the highest nominal GDP of any African nation, and with less than 100,000 people, it is the least populous African sovereign state.
- The Caribbean Islands are often known as the "Antilles" and are sub-divided into the "Greater Antilles" and "Lesser Antilles." The Greater Antilles include the larger islands of Cuba, Jamaica, Puerto Rico, and Hispaniola, while the Lesser Antilles include the Bahamas and the smaller island nations and colonies.
- The term "Antilles" is derived from the word "Antillia," which is a mysterious or lost island.
- The Cook Islands is a small archipelago in the South Pacific whose political status is a bit of a mixture. The Cook Islands are for the most part independent, but technically they are still reliant upon New Zealand for military defense. Cook Islanders are nationals of the Cook Islands but also New Zealand citizens.
- If you're ever in the Bahamas, you may want to check out Big Major Cay. If you make it there, be sure to visit Pig Beach, where you'll find swine happily swimming in the clear blue Caribbean waters!
- The Hawaiian Islands were a sovereign state from 1795 until 1893 when it was the Kingdom of Hawaii. From 1893 until 1898, it was the Republic of Hawaii, after which it became an American territory.

- Today Venice is a city in the sovereign state of Italy, but for much of its history, it was the independent Republic of Venice. The city and former republic are distributed across 118 islands.
- New Zealand's two primary islands are appropriately named North Island and South Island. In addition to the two primary islands, New Zealand claims more than 600 smaller islands for a total landmass of 103,500 square miles.
- Bikini Atoll, where the United States military conducted atomic weapons tests after World War II, is part of the now-sovereign state of the Marshall Islands.

POLAR OPPOSITES

On the very top and the very bottom of the Earth are the poles, where the planet's axis of rotation intersects the Earth. Of course, we know these as the North and South poles or the Arctic and Antarctic, respectively. Although the poles have many similarities, they are also quite different.

Both poles are the coldest places on Earth, but Antarctica is much colder on average. Low temperatures of -128 °F have been recorded, while the lowest in the Arctic is -90 °F. Antarctica is also quite dry and is considered a polar desert with less than eight inches of snow on the coastline per year on average and much less in the interior. Most areas of the Arctic receive about twice the amount of snowfall on average by comparison.

Perhaps one of the biggest differences between the two poles is the amount of land area. Antarctica is a continent—the fifth-largest—with more than 5.5 million square miles of area. On the other hand, the North Pole is actually in the middle of the Arctic Ocean with most of its land lying just inside the Arctic Circle with an Area of approximately 5.4 million sq. mi. which is largely frozen ocean.

Other than some researchers, Antarctica is devoid of human settlement, but the Arctic has a long history of permanent human activity. Besides being settled for such a long time, the Arctic has also been settled by a diverse range of different people, including Scandinavians, Russians, Saamis, and other indigenous Siberian peoples, plus various Inuit tribes. The term "Arctic" is derived from the Greek word *arktos*, which means "bear." The northern constellations of Ursa Major and Minor (the bears) pointed the way north for travelers, who eventually began referring to the far northern lands as "the Arctic."

The name "Antarctica" literally means "below the Arctic," perhaps not just indicating its geographic position, but also its relative importance in history. British explorer James Cook (1728-1779), who is famous for exploring Australia, theorized there was an equivalent of the North Pole in the Southern Hemisphere, but he was unable to find it. Finally, in 1820, a Russian exploration team led by Fabian Bellingshausen (1778-1852) and Mikhail Lazarev (1788-1851) sighted Antarctica. It wouldn't be until the 20th century, though, that there were major expeditions to explore the continent.

Both regions have different species of pinnipeds (seals), although their ranges are limited. For instance, the Arctic is best known for walruses, while Antarctica has plenty of Wedell seals. But, of course, when you think of cold weather animals, you think of penguins and polar bears, right? Polar bears are exclusive to the Arctic while penguins, of which there are several species, are limited to the Southern Hemisphere. The only way polar bears and penguins will ever meet is in a person's imagination or at a zoo!

Random Facts:

- Since the Earth's rotation is not fixed precisely, the geographic poles are technically different from the magnetic poles. The magnetic poles are also always moving, up to several feet in a year.
- Antarctica is defined as the land and ice shelves south of 60°S latitude.
- Depending on the season, Antarctica has a human population of 1,000 to 5,000 people. The winter months, which would be the summer months in the northern hemisphere, are when the fewest people live on the continent.
- Most of the vegetation in the Arctic consists of grasses, mosses, and dwarf shrubs. Most of the Arctic is tundra, so trees are not native to the region.
- The North Pole and the Arctic Ocean are neutral territories, with the Arctic nations being limited through a treaty to a 230-mile exclusive economic zone off their coasts.
- Only 5% of Antarctica's coastline is rock. The rest of the coastline is either: ice shelves, ice walls, or glacier outlets, which means that options to land on the continent via ship are limited and virtually impossible during the winter months.
- Those living near either pole have the similar fortune of being able to view the "northern lights" or "southern lights." Known scientifically as the aurora borealis (northern lights) or Aurora Australis (southern lights), these beautiful lights are the result of solar winds creating electrical discharges in the magnetosphere.
- Seven countries currently claim territory in Antarctica: France, the United Kingdom, New Zealand, Australia, Norway, Argentina, and Chile. Several more countries, including Russia, the United States, and Japan, have or have had researchers on the continent.

- The North Pole is warmer than the South Pole because it is at sea level and is not an island.
- The Antarctic Treaty System (ATS) is a treaty that was signed by 12 countries with claims and/or interests in Antarctica in 1959 and effective from 1961. The Treaty bans military and mining activity on Antarctica, essentially making the continent a neutral science zone.
- Scientists believe that the ice is melting at both poles, but that it's happening more rapidly at the North Pole.
- Arctic ice is thicker than Antarctic ice because of the nature of the geography of the two poles. The North Pole is surrounded by land, so when the ice sheet melts in the summer months, it is harder for chunks to break off and move south. As a result, the ice tends to accumulate and get harder. On the other hand, Antarctica is one giant landmass, so when the ice breaks away from the continent in the summer months, it can freely float north.
- The Arctic was explored fairly early. Norse/Viking expeditions sailed around the northern end of Scandinavia by 1000 CE, well within the Arctic Circle. Russians began exploring the Arctic region by the 1600s and in the 1700s the British began searching for a northwest passage through Arctic Canada to Asia.
- If you ever happen to visit Antarctica and enter the continent at Taylor Glacier, be sure to check out Blood Falls. This is an outflow of iron-oxide enriched salt water, which makes it look like a bloody waterfall flowing into the ocean.
- Norwegian Roald Amundsen (1872-c. 1928) is often considered one of the world's last great explorers and was crucial to the scientific understanding of both poles. Amundsen was the first person to successfully navigate the Northwest Passage by ship from 1903-1906. He then led the first successful expedition to the South Pole in 1911. He also led the first recorded flight over the North Pole in a dirigible (blimp) in 1926.

- Although the most recognizable animals from both polar regions will never meet, scientists have discovered more than 200 smaller marine organisms that live at both poles.
- Like the Arctic, Antarctica is devoid of trees. It has few plants as well, consisting mainly of mosses.
- Because the North Pole is over water, crossing it on land has been extremely difficult and is usually only done over two seasons. Explorers Ranulph Fiennes and Charles Burton were the first to traverse the North Pole by foot and with the use of open whaler boats in 1982.
- The Commonwealth Trans-Antarctic Expedition of 1955-1958 was the first expedition to successfully traverse Antarctica.
- In 2016, the *Crystal Serenity* became the first large cruise ship to navigate the Northwest Passage. The cruise was a 29-day journey from Vancouver, British Columbia to New York, New York via the Arctic which has since been cancelled as a trip.

THE EARTH IS MAINLY WATER

Well, that is sort of true. The surface of the Earth is 71% water-covered with over 96% of that being in the oceans. There is also water floating in the atmosphere as vapor and there is plenty of it beneath the surface in aquifers. If you combine *all* water on, in, and above the Earth, it would cover a 332,500,000 cubic miles. Now, that may sound like a lot, and it is, but it is nothing when you consider that the Earth's volume is 260 *billion* cubic miles!

The combined surface and underground water on Earth are enough to keep life going thanks to the hydrologic or water cycle. Water from the surface condenses into vapor, goes into the clouds, comes back to the Earth in the form of rain or snow, and then seeps into the ground, feeding the aquifers and surface bodies of water.

Scientists consider there to be one "World Ocean" and five subsidiary oceans: the Atlantic, Pacific, Indian, Arctic, and Southern/Antarctic. Some scientists consider the Antarctic Ocean to be an outlet of the Atlantic, Indian, and Pacific oceans, while other scientists consider the Arctic Ocean to be a sea of the Atlantic.

A sea is a large—usually salt water—body of water that is not as big as an ocean. Seas are defined loosely by different scholars, but they are generally a large bay or inlet of an ocean. Many seas, such as the Baltic, Mediterranean, and Black Seas, are virtually enclosed and separated from their oceans and other bodies of water by straits. Other seas, like the Caribbean Sea, are more open and are divided from the adjoining ocean by an archipelago.

A lake is a landlocked body of water located in a basin. The surface water in a lake is generally still, although they often have outlets or inlets. Lakes can contain salt or fresh water, or both, but unlike rivers, the precise definition is unclear. Some swamps and small ponds are considered lakes, as is the Caspian Sea, technically. Although the

Caspian Sea is called a "sea" and has a salinity of over 1%, it is also an inland body of water with no outlet or inlet to an ocean, so it is therefore can be considered as a lake.

The definition of a river is quite straight forward; the difference between a river and a stream/creek/brook is a bit of a gray area.

Random Facts:

- The Last Glacial Period took place about 115,000 years ago and ended approximately 11,700 years ago, leaving much of what is now Northern Europe, Canada, and the Northern United States under a sheet of ice. The retreat of the ice left thousands of new rivers and lakes in its wake.
- The Nile River, which flows through Egypt and ten other northeast African nations, was considered to be the longest in the world at 4,258 miles long. The Amazon River of South America is now considered to be the longest at 4,350miles long with the latest measurements, but it blows the Nile away in terms of the drainage area and total discharge.
- Lake Victoria, which lies across five southern African nations, is Africa's largest lake by volume, the world's largest tropical lake, the world's second-largest freshwater lake in surface area after Lake Superior, and the largest lake in the Southern Hemisphere—although the northern tip of the lake is in the Northern Hemisphere.
- A gulf is a body of water that is a large inlet from a larger body of water into a landmass and can be thought of as a large bay. If you follow the strictest definition, the Gulf of Mexico is the largest in the world, with a coastline of more than 3,100 miles and a surface area of more than 600,000 square miles. If you use a more liberal definition, though, the Bay of Bengal has more than 6,000 miles of coastline and a surface area of 839,000 square miles. The Hudson Bay in Canada has a shoreline of nearly 7,500 miles and a surface area of 470,000 square miles.
- Lake Agassiz was a large glacial lake that covered most of what is now Manitoba and parts of Ontario, Saskatchewan, North Dakota, and Minnesota 13,000 years ago. When it finally receded at the

end of the last glaciation, it left behind Lake Winnipeg, Lake Manitoba, and Lake Winnipegosis in Manitoba, and Rainy Lake, Red Lake, and Lake of the Woods in Minnesota.

- The Pacific Ocean is the largest in terms of area, volume, and coastline. It is also the deepest ocean on average.
- The Persian Gulf is an extension of the Indian Ocean that sits between Iran and the Arabian Peninsula.
- Unlike most major American rivers, the Red River of the North flows north, emptying in Lake Winnipeg, Manitoba.
- The Ogallala Aquifer is a large, underground freshwater lake in the Great Plains of the United States. It lies underneath parts of eight states, covering an area of about 174,000 square miles.
- The term "Seven Seas" has been used for centuries by different countries, although there was never a consensus on the list. Medieval European sources included the Adriatic Sea, the Mediterranean Sea, the Black Sea, the Caspian Sea, the Arabian Sea, the Red Sea, and the Persian Gulf. The medieval Islamic sources considered the Seven Seas to be the Persian Gulf, the Arabian Sea, the Bay of Bengal, the Strait of Malacca, the Singapore Strait, the Gulf of Thailand, and the South China Sea.
- Most of the major cities of the world are located on or near a major body of water.
- As a collective, the Great Lakes of North America are the largest group of freshwater lakes by total area and second largest in total volume. The Great Lakes were formed during the last glaciation, which in North America is known as the "Wisconsin glaciation."
- The Roe River in Montana held the title of "World's Shortest River" in the *Guinness Book of World Records* at 201 feet. The category was eventually eliminated, which is good for the Roe because the Reprua River in the Gagra District of Abkhazia would now have that title at only 89 feet in length.

- The Salton Sea in Southern California is a large, saline lake. It's located directly on top of the San Andreas fault line.
- The Arctic Ocean is the smallest and shallowest of the five oceans in terms of area, volume, and depth, but it has more than twice the shoreline of the Antarctic Ocean.
- A rift lake is a lake that is formed by the movement of the earth in a fault zone. The Dead Sea in Israel is perhaps one of the world's most famous rift lakes.
- The Bering Sea separates Russia from Alaska, but it didn't exist during the last glacial period. People moved across the Bering land bridge and populated the Americas until the ice receded.
- Lake Baikal in Siberia is the oldest and largest freshwater lake in the world by volume. It is home to the only exclusively freshwater seal species, the Baikal seal.
- An endorheic lake is a lake with no outlet to larger bodies of water. These lakes are usually saline, which limits aquatic life. The Great Salt Lake and the Caspian Sea are two of the best known endorheic lakes.
- Large amounts of water are located inside the Earth's crust, mantle, and core. Some scientists believe that the Earth's core could have five oceans worth of hydrogen alone!

THE WORLD WIDE WEB

There are a lot of things that help make a society and civilization function properly, but few things do so more on a practical level than transportation. As the world's population grows every increasingly bigger, the planet gets smaller, which can be attributed in a large part to transportation. We can get on a plane and travel across the planet within hours, efficient trains are common in many countries, and the lowered costs of automobiles have made it easier for more and more people to travel where they want and when they want.

Trains may be the primary way to move goods in most countries, but in North America (United States, Canada, and Mexico), trucks account for nearly 60% of all freight transportation. Sure, to ships goods over continents you need ships and/or planes, but as roads and vehicle technology have improved, the costs of shipping by trucks has decreased. Because of this, and due to the overall population increase in the world, more and more nations are connecting their people with highways.

The United States Interstate Highway system began in the 1950s as a Cold War project that would allow the rapid deployment of military units across the country. Before too long, Americans began using the interstates for leisure and business travel and companies found them perfect for shipping. Today, similar highway systems can be found all over Europe, parts of Asia, Australia, Latin America, and even some parts of Africa.

As technology progressed, the idea of connecting continents via highways became more popular in the mid-20th century.

In 1923, which was during a period of great optimism in the world, the idea of building a continuous highway, known as the "Pan-American Highway," from northern most Alaska to the southern tip of Argentina was proposed at the Fifth International Conference of

American States. The road was realized to a certain extent, although uneven funding and development in the various countries—and a big impediment called the Darién Gap (the Darien Gap is a remote, road-less swath of jungle on the border of Panama & Colombia) – which has so far kept it from becoming a complete reality.

Chances are, no matter where you are in the world, you can get in a car and go on a nice road trip on some fairly decent roads.

Random Facts:

- Germany's autobahn is among the oldest and most efficient highway systems in the world. It's a multilane highway system similar to the US Interstate system, although in Germany speed limits are optional in many rural areas. The autobahn system was begun by the Nazis as a public works/unemployment program.
- A divided highway is simply a highway that has multiple lanes for traffic going in opposite directions. Typically, there is a ditch or divider in the middle of the highway separating the opposite moving lanes. Divided highways with exit and entrance ramps are considered "controlled access" highways.
- If you plan to do some road tripping around the world, be aware that the color of highway guide signs (number of miles/kilometers to the next exit) varies from region to region. Most countries use green, but Western Europe is known for using blue on its major highways/carriageways. South Africa also uses blue on its freeway guide signs.
- At more than 3,500 miles, the Chinese highway numbered G010 was the longest highway in the country until it was abolished in 2016 by being re-designed into several highways.
- The Trans-African Highway network of 35,221 miles, is a series of roads that are meant to link every region of Africa: North, West, Central, East, and South. More than half the network is paved, although very few sections are divided highways. Drivability on the unpaved sections depends on seasonal rains, local maintenance, and political/social instability, so check ahead if you're planning on road tripping through Africa.
- The Australian highway system is similar to the United States', in that the most important highways are administered by the federal government, while the secondary highways are numbered and

maintained by the states. Freeways are also called "motorways" or "expressways" in Australia.

- Australian highways follow the British model and drivers are on the left hand side of the roadway. The US highways have right hand side drivers.
- Although it comprises more than one highway, the Trans-Canadian Highway is the longest highway within a single country in North America. It spans all ten Canadian provinces for 4,860 miles.
- The Lincoln Highway was first constructed in 1913 as the United States' first trans-national highway. It stretched from New York City to San Francisco and when it was (almost) completed in 1924, it was 3,124 miles now currently 3,389 miles fully completed.
- The Pan-American Highway may be the longest road in the world at more than 19,000 miles, but the Darién Gap will probably ensure that it's never quite completed. The Darién Gap is a heavy jungle and marshland in Panama and Colombia that causes a 70-mile break in the highway.
- The nomenclature used to describe divided highways differs widely from country to country and sometimes even within a country. In North America, controlled-access highways are called "freeways," "expressways," and often just as "highways." In the United Kingdom, though, they are referred to as "dual carriageways."
- If you're ever driving through Southern Minnesota on Interstate 90, make sure to stop in Blue Earth, Minnesota, where you'll be greeted by a 50-foot statue of the "Jolly Green Giant." The Giant was constructed to commemorate the completion of Interstate 90 in Minnesota in 1978, which joined other interstates, creating a continuous interstate corridor from coast to coast.
- National Highway 44 is the longest in India at 2,365 miles.

- The Asian Highway Network is a series of numbered highways that connect 32 Asian countries, including Russia. The purpose of the network is to better facilitate trade and tourism, especially in the less developed countries of South and Southeast Asia.
- The Trans-Siberian Highway runs the entire length of Russia, east to west, for 6,800 miles. Like most of the other longest highways in the world, it's a combination of several highways.
- Freeway/highway/interstate exits are generally marked sequentially from where the highway begins in a state to where it ends. Beginning in the 1960s in the United States, the numbers began to reflect mileage, which made it easier for travelers. Most countries with extensive freeway systems also number exits, although they reflect kilometers, not miles, of course.
- The earliest highways of significance were built by the Egyptians in the Late Bronze Age (1,500-1,200 BCE), after which the Persians improved on the idea in the 6th century BC by adding motels along their roads, among other amenities. The Romans were the first people to use "mile markers" and concrete to build roads.
- Highway 1 is Australia's transnational highway. It wraps around the island nation in a 9,000-mile loop.
- The Ba Nang Expressway has the longest automobile bridge in the world. If you suffer from Gephyrophobia (fear of bridges), you may want to stay away from Ba Nang because the bridge spans 34 miles!
- The South African highway system, called and marked as "National routes," was based on the American interstate system and built in the 1970s. If you're an American and happen to visit and drive in South Africa, you may be amazed at how similar the highways systems are. There is one notable difference you better not forget though—they drive on the left side in South Africa!
- Interstate 80 replaced the Lincoln Highway. Construction on Interstate 80 first began in 1956 and was finally completed in 1986.

SIZE ISN'T EVERYTHING

Earlier in this book, we did an overview of the world's sovereign states and also met some of the largest countries in physical size and population. It should've been immediately apparent that the largest countries of the world pack a heavy punch in terms of political, economic, social, and cultural influence. The largest countries have the highest GDP, the largest militaries, and can influence the rest of the world with their sheer numbers and size.

But that isn't to say that the smallest countries aren't important.

Many of the world's smallest sovereign states are defined as "microstates." A microstate is generally defined as a country with both a small area and population, although some microstates only qualify in one of those categories. For instance, Singapore is quite small in land area—with only 276 square miles, it is ranked 175 among all sovereign states—but is in the middle of the ranking in population with 5.7 million people.

On the other hand, the Scandinavian island nation of Iceland certainly fits the microstate definition in population with only 317,351 people, but its nearly 40,000 square miles of landmass makes it the 106th largest sovereign state.

The smallest sovereign state in terms of both physical size and population is Vatican City, but it's undeniable that the center of the Roman Catholic Church has a great deal of influence throughout the world. Sure, there are only about 1,000 Vatican City passport holders, the country is surrounded by Italy, and is less than half a square mile, but 1.3 billion people around the world look to that tiny country for spiritual leadership.

No matter their status in terms of world politics, economics, or culture, all of the world's smallest nations are the most important places to their citizens. The people of the world's microstates report some of the highest levels of satisfaction with their governments and less internal social conflict.

Random Facts:

- Tuvalu is the fourth-smallest sovereign state in physical size and third-smallest in population. Just over 11,802 people live on the tiny South Pacific atoll nation, which is known for its sandy beaches and Polynesian culture.
- The island nation of Saint Kitts and Nevis is the smallest sovereign state in North America in both landmass and population.
- Monaco is the second-smallest European nation, occupying less than a square mile on the French Mediterranean coast. Like most of the other European microstates, Monaco's government is a constitutional monarchy.
- Belize is the smallest country in continental North America in population with just over 408,407 people. Although it is located in the heart of Spanish-speaking Central America, Belize was a long-time British colony so today English is its official language.
- The European microstate of Malta is the smallest member of the European Union.
- Many of the world's microstates are in the South Pacific, which is a region known as Oceania.
- Unlike a microstate, which is a sovereign state, a micro nation is a political entity that has claimed sovereign status over a small area within or at the edge of an existing country but has not been granted it and/or has not been recognized by other states or the United Nations. Micro nations are different from full-fledged secessionist movements because they are rarely violent and are seldom taken seriously by the relevant governments.
- Unlike Europe, Asia, and Oceania, Africa has few microstates. Located in the Indian Ocean off the coast of East Africa, Seychelles is an archipelago with only 176 square miles of land and less than 100,000 people. It is the smallest African nation.

- If Oceania nations are not included, the Maldives is the smallest country in size and population in Asia. In case you're wondering, the Maldives (115 sq. miles) is located on the southwest tip of India in the Indian Ocean.
- There are a total of six microstates in Europe: Andorra, Lichtenstein, Monaco, San Marino, Vatican City, and Malta.
- Although not considered a microstate, Luxemburg is pretty small. The landlocked Western European country has a total area of just under 1,000 square miles and a population of 626,451.
- Although predominantly Spanish-speaking Puerto Rico isn't an independent state, it has less landmass than any Spanish-speaking country in the Americas.
- The Gambia is the smallest sized sovereign state in continental Africa, but Djibouti is the least populous country on the mainland with 884,017 people.
- El Salvador is the smallest country in size in continental North America, at 8,124 square miles, beating out Belize by about 700 miles.
- Suriname (located on the northern coast of South America) is the smallest South American country in size and population. It has a landmass of 63,250 square miles and a population of 581,000. Suriname is culturally very different than other South American countries: most of the people speak Dutch, Asian Indians comprise the largest ethnic group, and Hindus are more than 20% of the population.
- Panama is generally considered the smallest neighboring transcontinental sovereign state, as most of it is in North America, but its southern edge is in South America. Some argue that Georgia, which is slightly smaller in land mass, should have the honor but whether any of it is in Europe has been debated.
- With only 8.1 square miles of landmass, the sovereign state of

Nauru is the smallest island nation and republic in the world. It is also the second-smallest nation in population (10,670) , but number three is the neighboring South Pacific nation of Tuvalu (11,802)

- Lebanon is the 7th smallest country in Asia in landmass and population, but it has the highest number of Christians per capita (40.57%).
- The smallest country in mainland East Asia (which doesn't include Middle Eastern countries) in terms of land area is Taiwan, with 13,826 square miles.
- The smallest country size-wise in all of Asia is The Maldives, then the next smallest continental Asian country is Singapore.

JUST FOR FUN

Now that you have a better sense of the size of our planet and where things are located, let's take a look at some of the top tourist destinations on Earth. When I say "top" destinations here, I don't just mean in terms of sheer numbers, although that's important and will be considered. I also mean a location's cultural and economic importance to the region and the world. Once we get past the numbers, it's truly a subjective matter concerning what type of places people like to visit during their vacations.

Historically important vacation destinations are popular. For example, nearly 15 million people from around the world travel to Egypt every year to visit the only extant monument from the Seven Wonders of the Ancient World, as well as 3,000 plus tombs and temples scattered throughout the country. More than ten million people travel to see the Great Wall of China annually and more than 1.2 million make the trek into the Andes Mountains to see Machu Picchu.

If enjoying the sun and the sand is more your thing while on vacation, then there is a beach for you on every continent except for Antarctica. Millions of people flock to the beaches of Florida and Hawaii daily to fish, surf, and sunbath, but if you want something more exotic, the island nation of Fiji may be your place. More than 890,000 people visit Fiji every year to enjoy some of the friendliest beaches in the South Pacific.

Ecotourism is also becoming a popular type of tourism and in the Central American nation of Costa Rica, many companies are combining that trend with extreme sports and people's love of beaches. In Costa Rica, you can ride a zip line over the rainforest canopy and have a freshly made local coffee on the beach all before noon!

If you're a bit of a risk-taker, there are plenty of gambling destinations. In the United States, Las Vegas and Atlantic City aren't the only gambling destinations anymore. Most American states have some type of legalized gambling; in fact, most countries in the world do as well. Other than Vegas, Monte Carlo, Monaco, and Macau, China is known around the world for its top casino destinations.

So, whether your thing is museums, amusement parks, or natural beauty, there is probably something nearby your home worth seeing.

Random Facts:

- The Magic Kingdom, known better as Disney World, is the most-attended amusement park in the world with over 52 million visitors to all sites. More than 21 million people walk through the gates every year to ride Space Mountain and see Mickey, Minnie, and Goofy.
- If you're a devout Roman Catholic, especially of Mexican ancestry, then the Basilica of Our Lady of Guadalupe just north of Mexico City is a top destination. The church is visited by more than 20 million people every year. They come to see the cloak they believe depicts the image of the Virgin of Guadalupe.
- The American amusement park company "Six Flags" owns more theme parks than any other company in the world. In addition to its dozens of amusement parks and water parks scattered throughout the United States, Six Flags operates theme parks in Canada and Mexico. Six Flags Mexico is the most popular theme park in Latin America, with more than 2.5 million people attending the park annually.
- As many as 17,000 visitors drive down Lombard Street in San Francisco, California every day. Well, not all of Lombard Street—just a one-block section near downtown that is billed as the "crookedest street in the world."
- Bali, Indonesia is a unique province of Indonesia and a major tourist attraction. The majority Hindu province is known for its friendly locals, happening nightclubs, and excellent surfing beaches.
- In addition to the Magic Kingdom and the original Disneyland Park in California, there are Disneyland theme parks in Paris, Tokyo, Hong Kong, and Shanghai.
- The definition of "ecotourism" is a bit fluid as several different

organizations have definitions of their own, but most agree that it involves tourism that allows people to view flora and fauna in their natural habitat while leaving minimal to no impact.

- "Safari" is a Swahili word meaning "journey." The term was first used for trips taken by Europeans, and later Americans, to Africa in the late 1800s and early 1900s to big game hunt.
- France attracts more than 89.4 million tourists every year, making it the number one national tourist destination in the world.
- Although Thailand is generally a safe and stable country, it recorded the most American tourist deaths per capita in 2019. Part of the reason for this statistic is the general "party atmosphere" of the country, the easy availability of alcohol and drugs, and other "shady" activities that Americans engage in when they visit Thailand.
- Niagara Falls is consistently at the top of many lists of most-visited tourist attractions in the world. The general location combines natural beauty with kitsch and casinos to offer something for everyone.
- Beto Carreo World is the largest amusement park in South America and Latin America. Located in the southern Brazilian state of Santa Catarina, Beto Carreo World is subdivided into seven themed sections over a 5.4 square mile area.
- You may find this hard to believe, but Lebanon was once a popular tourist destination among Europeans. The beaches, casinos, generally tolerant religious attitudes among the natives, and cheap prices compared to Europe attracted millions of people until the Lebanese Civil War (1975-1990) broke out, forever scarring the small Middle Eastern nation.
- There is no better place to go snorkeling than the Great Barrier Reef off the coast of Queensland, Australia. More than two million people from around the world visit the Reef every year to see the incredible marine ecosystem.

- Built in the mid-5th century BCE, the Temple of Athena in the Acropolis of Athens was built to showcase Athens' dominance of the Greek city-states. Today, it's the main ancient historical tourist destination in Europe, drawing more than four million visitors annually. Greece records over 34 million visitors per year.
- About 2.3 million people visit Iceland every year. Although technically a European country, Iceland is known more for its majestic mountains, volcanoes, geysers, and springs than its architecture or monuments.
- Due to its immense physical size and lenient gun laws, the United States is a prime hunting destination for foreign tourists as well as Americans.
- From the 1960s through the 1980s, Americans flocked to Acapulco, Mexico's resorts, but due to cartel violence and general crime, it was a shell of its former self by the late 2000s. The area around Cancun on the Yucatan Peninsula is now Mexico's resort hot spot.
- If you're a wine connoisseur with a little money, you have plenty of excellent options. If pinot noir or chardonnay is your thing then the Burgundy region of France is a must-see, while the Campania in Italy also won't disappoint. There are also plenty of good wine regions closer to home, namely the Wine Country of the Napa and Sonoma valleys of California.
- Disneyland Paris may be the most popular theme park in Europe, but a close second is Europa-Park in Germany. Europa-Park is known for its 13 rollercoasters, which attract 5.7 million people in 2017 to the park.

CHAPTER 2:

Pop Culture Around the World

THE TRIPLE CROWN OF AMERICAN ACTING

You've probably heard of the Triple Crown of horse racing? The Kentucky Derby, the Belmont Stakes, and the Preakness are the most-watched races with the biggest purses, with the goal of every horse and rider being to win all three in one year.

Did you know that American film and television also has a triple crown?

The top three awards in American film are the following: the Academy Award (Oscar) for film, the Emmy Award for television, and the Tony for theater. Since all three genres of acting require very different skill-sets and experiences, the American acting triple crown has only been won 24 times.

It can also often take an actor a lifetime to win the triple crown. Due to the nature of professional acting, schedules are set up months or years in advance and actors tend to focus on one genre throughout their careers.

For instance, British actress Glenda Jackson became the most recent winner of the triple crown when she won the Tony Award in 2018.

She had previously won the Academy Award in 1971 for best actress for her role in the film *Women in Love* and the Emmy Award in 1972 for the series *Elizabeth R*.

Although all three awards are given by American associations, they are not limited to American actors or American productions.

Random Facts:

- The Academy Award is awarded by the Academy of Motion Picture Arts and Sciences. The award was first given in 1927-28.
- British actor Paul Schofield (1922-2008) completed the acting triple crown in the fewest years (seven). Primarily a stage actor, Schofield won the Tony in 1962, the Oscar in 1967, and the Emmy in 1969.
- American actor Thomas Mitchell and American actress Helen Hayes were the first two people—and first man and woman, respectively—to win the triple crown in 1953. It took Hayes 21 years to achieve the feat and Mitchel 13.
- The Tony Award is an abbreviation of the Antoinette Perry Award for Excellence in Broadway Theatre. It was first awarded in 1947.
- Brad Pitt, Matt Damon, and Robert DeNiro have all won plenty of acting awards, but none have won the triple crown.
- The Emmy Award was first given in 1949. Since television is so much bigger than film or theater in terms of viewers and genres, there are several Emmy ceremonies at different times of the year. The biggest Emmy award ceremonies are for the Primetime Emmy Awards and the Daytime Emmy Awards.
- Fifteen women and nine men have won the acting triple crown.
- The Academy Award is usually referred to as an "Oscar" because that is the name of the statue that is given as a trophy. The trophy was first called Oscar in 1939, although the origin of the name is not certain.
- Viola Davis became the first Black actor to win the triple crown in 2017. She won the Tony in 2001, the Emmy in 2015, and the Oscar in 2017.

- The Daytime Emmy Awards are dominated by soap operas. Soap star Susan Lucci was nominated for 18 Emmys before finally winning in 1999, though she has never won the triple crown.

- British actress Maggie Smith has won the most number of the three coveted awards with seven. It took her 33 years to reach this number, after earning an Emmy in 2003.

- In addition to winning the acting triple crown, entertainers Helen Hayes and Rita Moreno have also won Grammy Awards, which sets them apart from all other actors.

- British actress Helen Mirren won the triple crown in 2015 and she is the only person to have won the British equivalent: a British Academy Film Award, British Academy Television Award, and an Olivier Award.

- Australian actor Geoffrey Rush was the youngest person to win the acting triple crown at the age of 57, while Glenda Jackson was the oldest at 82.

- The Emmy trophy is probably almost as recognizable as the Oscar. It's a 15.5 inch tall copper, nickel, silver, and gold statue of a winged woman holding an atom.

- Al Pacino is probably the most "popular" and big-name box office star to have won the triple crown. Pacino won a Tony for best featured actor in 1969 for the play *Does a Tiger Wear a Necktie?* He then won an Oscar in 1993 for best actor in *Scent of a Woman* and completed the cycle by winning a Primetime Emmy for his role in the 2003 HBO miniseries *Angels in America.*

- All three awards ceremonies are broadcast on live television, with the Oscars by far being the most watched and the Tony's being the least-watched.

- Since the Emmy Awards are given for excellence in television, the ceremony is generally rotated among the four major American television networks. It's usually broadcast on a Sunday night

before the fall television season begins.

- Due to a perception of many classically trained actors that television is "lowbrow," acting triple crown winners often get their Emmy in a BBC production or, in more recent years, on HBO. For 15 of the 24 winners, the Emmy was the last of the three trophies won.
- Legendary Swedish actress Ingrid Bergman (1915-1982) was the third person to win the acting triple crown in 1960. She completed the cycle by winning a Primetime Emmy for a guest starring role in the anthology series *Startime*.

THEY CALL IT K-POP

Since World War II, the United States has been the center of the pop culture world, exporting its creations to the farthest corners of the globe. Hollywood was exporting its productions even before World War II, but after the war, with the emergence of dubbing and subtitles, American movies began being consumed by just about every country.

American music has also been exported to people around the world, especially the youth, but sometimes the influence happens the other way.

The British rock band The Beatles were the first in a wave known as the "British Invasion," which was a series of British bands that became popular in the US. Later, there was a "Latin Explosion" in the 1990s when salsa influenced acts like Ricky Martin hit the top of the charts and today we're experiencing a possibly even bigger foreign pop phenomenon—K-pop.

K-pop refers to Korean pop music, and at first glance, it looks and sounds a lot like American/Western pop music. The music is heavy on electronics and is often catchy and danceable, although for the most part unintelligible to anyone who doesn't know Korean.

The most popular K-pop performers are the "idol" groups, which feature groups of pretty young women or men doing highly choreographed acts. Although K-pop performers have genuine musical and dancing talent, and usually come from musical backgrounds, they are carefully chosen by music companies.

Once the performers get too old for the idol bands, they are dropped or the entire group is disbanded. Typically, K-pop idol bands usually don't last much longer than five years.

K-pop's popularity spread across Asia in the 1990s and then into Asian enclaves in non-Asian countries in the 2000s. The success of

Korean artist Psy's "Gangnam Style" in 2012 brought K-pop to the attention of millions outside of Asia and now it is the fastest-growing musical genre in popularity in the world.

Chances are, no matter where you live, someone you know listens to K-pop.

Random Facts:

- The K-pop industry is very vertically integrated. Music companies control the recruitment and training of idols, the recording of music, the booking and scheduling of concerts and tours, as well as publicity and merchandizing.
- The three major K-pop companies are SM Entertainment, YG Entertainment, and JYP Entertainment.
- The boy band BTS (Bangtan Boys) is currently the best-selling K-pop band in the world. BTS was formed in 2010 by Big Hit Entertainment, debuted in 2013 and was immediately successful. They sold 2.7 million copies of their albums in 2017 and then nearly doubled that a year later by selling 5.15 million copies.
- K-pop is generally considered part of the larger phenomenon known as the "Korean Wave." The Korean Wave began in the 1990s and, besides K-pop, it includes the exporting of Korean movies and television shows, Korean food, and Korean clothing styles.
- Listening to or possessing K-pop is punishable by death in North Korea.
- The female idol band KARA had quite a long run relative to other K-pop groups. DSP Media formed KARA in 2007 and after a very successful nine-year run, Gyuri Park and Hara Goo decided not to renew their contracts in 2016, ending the band in the process.
- The idol groups are highly visual and very stylized, often changing their clothing during a concert. One of the more popular clothing styles worn by idol groups is the "street" style, which features performers wearing brightly colored clothing typical of South Korean fashion.
- The road to being a K-pop star is difficult and involves a process

known as "cultural technology." The stages of the process are casting, training, producing, and marketing. The lives of the idols are heavily regimented, with the management companies overseeing their diets, schedules, and social networks.

- In recent years, the K-pop industry has been beset by scandal, many centered on the management companies' exploitation of the performers. Some notable suicides of performers and former performers have also gripped K-pop, most notably by former KARA member Goo Hara/Hara Goo in 2019.
- The general term for the global spread of Korean pop culture is *Hallyu*. In 2018, there were more than 1,800 Hallyu fan clubs worldwide.
- K-pop has undoubtedly influenced global music, but it has also influenced global fashion in many ways. The "straight eyebrow" look was made popular throughout Asia by K-pop female idols and it is now becoming popular outside Asia.
- Due to World War II, South Korea had many restrictions on trade and diplomacy with Japan until the 1990s. The early K-pop girl group S.E.S. is often credited with thawing relations between the countries, debuting in Japan, and doing some songs in Japanese. Since that time, many K-pop bands record some of their songs in Japanese and often perform in Japanese when touring Japan.
- In 2009, the female K-pop group Wonder Girls was the first K-pop act to debut on the Billboard Hot 100 singles chart.
- K-pop songs often have English titles and may use English language phrases and refrains, but most of the lyrics are actually in Korean.
- Many K-pop idols have worked, lived, or are even from the United States. Shon Seung-wan—better known as Wendy—from the group Red Velvet, lived in Canada and the United States for most of her teen years. Mark, from the boy band Got7, was born in the United States.

- There has been a trend in recent years of K-pop idols from Japan, China, Taiwan, and Thailand, although they are often billed as being from South Korea. Three members of the girl band Twice are from Japan.
- K-pop emerged gradually beginning in the 1950s, but it always took a back seat to the Japanese J-pop style of music until the 1990s.
- Fan obsession and stalking can be such a problem for K-pop musicians that it even has a name of its own: *sasaeng*.
- Despite the official ban on K-pop in North Korea, dictator Kim Jong-un is said to be quite a fan of the genre. In 2018, the North Korean government hosted the first-ever K-pop concert in the capital city of Pyongyang, which was attended by Kim Jong-un.
- American audiences got their first taste of live K-pop at the Korean Music Festival, which began in 2003 at the Hollywood Bowl in Los Angeles. Solo male performer Rain was the first K-pop musician to sell out the American venues in 2006.

BOLLYWOOD

You probably think that Hollywood produces more feature films than any other country, but it only ranks third behind India and Nigeria. It makes sense if you think about it. With more than one billion people in India and a diaspora of many millions more scattered throughout the world, the Indian film industry has a naturally large fan base.

The Indian film industry is itself divided into three primary sub-industries that are based on language: Telegu film, Tamil film, and Bollywood. Bollywood is the largest, oldest, and most important of the three Indian film industries.

The term "Bollywood" is a portmanteau that combines "Bombay," now Mumbai, which is the headquarters of the film industry, with "Hollywood." The language used in Bollywood films is Hindustani, which is closely related to the Indo-European languages spoken in northern India and Pakistan.

With nearly 400 films released every year, Bollywood movies are as diverse in content as India is in languages and ethnic groups. Lighthearted romantic comedies are among the more popular genres of Bollywood films, but films that explore serious social problems and ideas are also common. Music plays a key role in Bollywood films, with actors often being expected to sing and dance as well as act.

Named for the popular spice mixture found in many Indian foods, "masala film" is a Bollywood genre that mixes action, comedy, romance, drama, and musicals into a style that—on first view—often seems confusing and somewhat humorous to non-Indians. A typical masala film may feature a humorous shootout between the protagonist and his rival and is interrupted by a musical routine.

It may seem strange to you, but the writers, directors, and actors of these films are laughing their way to the bank as they earn millions of rupees a year.

Random Facts:

- The 2008 British film *Slumdog Millionaire* is thought of by many as an example of a Bollywood-influenced masala-type film. The film had plenty of laughs, action, jokes, and romance, and even ended with a musical routine.
- Although Hindi is the primary language of most people in northern India, Hindustani is intelligible by native speakers as the former is derived from the latter. Native speakers of Urdu, which is the primary language in Pakistan, also understand Hindustani, placing Bollywood's cultural reach firmly in two primary countries.
- The most expensive Bollywood film of all time was the science fiction movie *Ra One* (2011). It cost approximately $US35 million to make.
- Although Bollywood films are extremely popular in Pakistan, the government bans their screening and telecasts due to its ongoing problems with India. Millions of Pakistanis continue to watch Bollywood films, though, via bootleg copies.
- Bollywood movies generally sell more tickets than their Hollywood counterparts but make less money. In 2002, Bollywood sold more than 3.6 billion tickets to Hollywood's 2.6 billion, but only brought in $1.3 billion in revenue to Hollywood's $51 billion.
- Early Bollywood history followed a similar course to Hollywood, although a little later. Bollywood's first "talkie" film was *Alam Ara* in 1931.
- You may recognize Priyanka Chopra from the American television series *Quantico*, or her recent role in movies such as *Baywatch*, but she got her start in Bollywood in the early 2000s.
- Salman Khan is considered the most recognizable and highest-

paid Bollywood star. He is the son of the well-known Bollywood screenwriter Salim Khan and is the brother of Bollywood actors Arbaaz and Sohail Khan.

- The term "Bollywood" was first coined in the 1970s, during Bollywood's classical or golden age.
- The masala films originated in the 1970s and were influenced by many different genres in India and Hollywood. Many of Hollywood's first sound films were musicals, which influenced the masala style.
- Although many Bollywood films are produced outside of India in countries with sizable Indian diaspora populations, non-Indians rarely land significant roles in the movies. The limited nature of Bollywood casting is also apparent within India, as the biggest name actors tend to be from the north and have lighter complexions.
- The music in Bollywood films is called "filmi."
- Suraiya Jamal Sheikh (1929-2004), better known by her mononym "Suraiya," was the Rita Hayworth of early Bollywood. Known for her beauty as well as her dancing and singing abilities, Suraiya appeared in 67 films from 1936 to 1963.
- Deepika Padukone is currently the most popular and one of the highest-paid actresses in Bollywood.
- Although the country of Bangladesh has its own Bengali language film industry, most native Bengali speakers can understand Hindustani so Bollywood films are quite popular in that country.
- A popular genre of Bollywood film that deals with issues in the Muslim communities is known as "Muslim social." It was popular from the 1950s until the 1970s but has made a modest resurgence in recent years.
- In the Soviet Union (1922-1991), Bollywood films were more

popular than heavily-censored Russian films and easier to come by than Hollywood films.

- Bootlegging is a problem for all film industries, but it is especially so for Bollywood. It's estimated that Bollywood loses more the $100 million a year to bootlegged copies of its movies.
- The 2016 film *Dangal* is the highest-grossing Bollywood film of all time, at over $300 million.
- Raj Kapoor (1924-1988) was a popular Bollywood actor in the 1950s and '60s who used a hobo persona that was based on Charlie Chaplin's "The Tramp."

TOO SEXY

As we continue on our journey through global pop culture trivia, you've no doubt noticed that there are some cultural elements that set these different eras and styles of entertainment apart. What works with K-pop might not necessarily work in Europe, while what worked in silent films won't sell tickets today. With that said, there is one thing that all successful pop cultural styles and phenomena have in common—distinct clothing styles.

Some people argue that pop culture is a reflection of society, while others say it is the primary influencer of society. When it comes to fashion, it certainly seems more like the latter than the former.

Most of you reading this have probably seen clips of major fashion shows and said to yourself, "no one ever wears those clothes." But there is a method, and plenty of money, behind what appears on face value to be fashion madness.

If you go beyond the over-the-top fall fashions, you'd realize that the fashion industry is pretty powerful and important in many countries. Four cities—Paris, London, New York, and Milan—are considered the primary fashion capitals of the world. These are the cities where the top designers live, where the top fashion shows are held, and where the models all flock to for work. There are also several secondary fashion capitals scattered throughout the world.

Random Facts:

- Medellin, Colombia is considered the fashion capital of Latin America.
- A "fashion house" is a company that makes high-end fashion. The term began in the 1800s when Charles Frederick Worth sewed his label onto his finished products. The term, along with so much of high-end fashion, originated in France from the term *maison couture*, or "fashion house."
- *Haute couture* (high fashion) refers to custom-fitted clothing. These are often the dresses you see at fashion shows and they are also the dresses and suits worn by celebrities at awards ceremonies.
- During the Cold War, fashion in the Soviet Union was often lampooned in the Western media. During Stalin's rule (1927-1953), fashion was severely regulated and the official stance prohibited workers from wearing stylish clothing. Although the reality was far from the image, after Stalin's death Soviet everyday fashions began to resemble those in the West.
- The combined value of the global fashion industry is more than $40 billion.
- Although Tokyo, Japan was the fashion capital of Asia for decades, it has recently been replaced by Shanghai, China.
- Italian brand Gucci is always one of the most popular high-end fashion labels and often gains the highest revenue. Gucci opened in 1921 in Florence, Italy and today it generates about $4 billion in revenue worldwide.
- Although not the largest city in Italy, Milan rose to prominence in the fashion world during the Renaissance (late 1400s-1600s), when designers in the city made clothing for the rich and powerful in Italy. A combination of enterprising entrepreneurs who called the

city their home, support for designers, and general fashion interest by the citizens made Milan a fashion capital by the late 1800s.

- For a city to be a fashion capital, it has to have high revenues in addition to several designers and fashion houses. New York, Paris, and London are all the financial capitals of their respective countries and are also media and entertainment centers.
- During the Weimar Period of Germany history (1920s), Berlin rivaled Paris and New York as a premier fashion capital.
- The Versace fashion company was founded by Gianni Versace in 1978 in Milan. Versace has been at the cutting edge of high-end fashion and consistently one of the top-selling fashion houses in the world. Gianni was murdered on July 15, 1997 at his Miami Beach home by spree killer Andrew Cunanan.
- An average fashion designer in New York City makes about $83,000 a year. Not bad, but not necessarily great either when you consider the high cost of living in the Big Apple. The real money in fashion is in owning a fashion house.
- "Fashion week" is a week-long event during which the industry's top designers and fashion house owners come together to show off their latest lines. The most notable fashion weeks take place in one of the four fashion capitals, although regional fashion capitals also have events of their own.
- "Prêt-à-porter" refers to "ready-to-wear" clothing made by a fashion house. Although not designed for specific individuals, ready-to-wear clothing is still very expensive and high-end.
- Sydney is the fashion capital of Australia and Oceania, although if considered as part of southeast Asia, then Singapore and Kuala Lumpur, Malaysia would have something to say.
- Nearly two million people in the United States are employed in the fashion industry, which is followed by approximately 555,000

employed in fashion in the United Kingdom, and about 340,000 people working in fashion in Germany and France.

- Mass market clothing is usually "last year's" stock of new fashions that the major fashion houses decide to mass-produce and sell in big-name retail stores.
- New York City rose to become one of the four major fashion capitals after World War II. The rise of American dominance after the war helped, as did the booming garment district in Manhattan and countless textile mills in the northeast.
- Gisele Bundchen was the highest-paid model in 2016, pulling down a cool $45 million! Most models, though—even those who work for the top fashion houses—make much less. The average New York model makes about $50,000, which is less than the average designer makes.
- Although Milan is the fashion capital of Italy and one of the four major fashion capitals, Florence is a close second and Rome is a not-so-distant third in Italy.
- Lagos, Nigeria is considered by many to be the fashion capital of Africa.

VIDEO KILLED THE RADIO STAR

When the Music Television network (MTV) launched on August 1, 1981, it was truly a major turning point in pop culture. The first video to play was "Video Killed the Radio Star" by the New Wave band the Buggles, and for a time, that seemed to be true. MTV played music videos for 24 hours for much of the 1980s and as the popularity of the network grew, so too did MTV's programming.

The continued popularity of music videos throughout the 1980s led MTV to diversify its programming: there was *120 Minutes* for fans of alternative music, *Headbangers Ball* for metal-heads, and *Yo! MTV Raps* for early hip hop aficionados. MTV became so popular that many American cable networks, such as USA and TBS, offered blocks of music video programming on Friday and Saturday nights and many local stations also got into the act by airing music video shows of their own.

There is no doubt that MTV and music videos in general influenced global pop culture in the 1980s. Videos unconsciously, or sometimes consciously, promoted all the latest fashion fads and they made words like "awesome," "nerd," and "grody" common across America.

Music videos also made many stars careers in the 1980s. Well-written and highly-choreographed videos, like the one for Michael Jackson's "Thriller," helped catapult many a rock star to celebrity status during the decade of excess.

But did video kill the radio star? It certainly seemed that way in the 1980s but less so today. Musicians continue to produce videos, but they play a less important role in defining a musician's success.

Random Facts:

- Bands and musicians filmed videos as promotions for albums as far back as the 1950s. Tony Bennet has claimed to have made the first music video for the 1956 song "Stranger in Paradise," although live songs filmed before that were later put into video format.
- To set themselves apart and show that it was different than radio, MTV referred to its on-air hosts as "VJs", short for "video jockey."
- *Night Flight* was a music-themed television series that aired on the cable network USA from 1981 to 1988. It aired on Friday and Saturday nights for four hours and featured a combination of music videos, B films, and interviews with musicians.
- Michael Jackson's "Thriller" video was unique for its time and still is, for several reasons. First, notable Hollywood director John Landis directed the video. Second, it was much longer than other videos at 14 minutes. Lastly, it cost $500,000 to make, which was an immense amount for the time.
- MuchMusic launched on August 31, 1984, as Canada's 24-hour music video channel.
- VJ Alan Hunter was the first person to speak on MTV when he said, "I'm Alan Hunter. I'll be with you right after Mark. We'll be covering the latest in music news, coast to coast, here on MTV Music Television."
- *Friday Night Videos* was a music video program that aired on NBC from 1983 to 2002. The show aired for 90 minutes throughout the 1980s and then 60 minutes from 1987 until it was canceled.
- Country Music Television (CMT) became the first cable network dedicated to country music when it launched on March 5, 1983.
- MTV Europe launched on August 1, 1987. The VJs spoke English,

but they were from every corner of the continent. Instead of kicking off with a video, MTV Europe began its programming with an Elton John live performance in London. The first video shown was Dire Straits' "Money for Nothing."

- The American television show *The Monkees* (1966-1968) experimented with early music videos. Each episode of the show would feature a song sung by the studio band, The Monkees, backed by a quirky music video.
- *Night Tracks* was the name of the weekend video music program on the American cable television channel TBS. The show would run for up to three hours, with its length depending on if Atlanta Braves baseball was broadcast that night, and was on the air from 1983 to 1992.
- The American cable network Black Entertainment Television (BET) launched in the 1980's, as a music video alternative to MTV. At the time, MTV played far fewer Black musicians, so BET filled that void.
- MTV had a difficult time getting off the ground during its first couple years of existence so it embarked on a memorable ad campaign where actors would tell viewers to call their local cable companies and proclaim, "I want my MTV!" MTV's studios were based in New York City when it first went on the air.
- Warner Communications, the company that originally owned MTV, launched the cable video music network Video Hits 1 (VH1) on January 1, 1985. While MTV's target demographic was teens, VH1 appealed to a slightly older and more urban demographic, playing more R&B, among other genres.
- Music video channels came a little later to Latin America. MTV Brasil debuted in 1990 and MTV Latin America went on the air in 1993.
- Just two days after CMT went on the air, The Nashville Network

(TNN) launched its brand as a country music video channel on March 7, 1983. Although TNN played music videos, it also offered a variety of shows that were popular with rural audiences.

- Marvin Gaye's "Star-Spangled Banner" was the first video aired on VH1.
- From its start to 2006, MTV was known for using the Kabel typeface to label its videos. VH1 also used the Kabel typeface on its videos.
- The 1995 Michael Jackson and Janet Jackson video for the song "Scream" is the most expensive video of all time. The adjusted cost of the video is $11,745,141.
- Along with Alan Hunter, the original MTV VJs included Mark Goodman, Nina Blackwood, Martha Quinn, and J.J. Jackson. The original VJs were paid in the mid-$20,000s, which wasn't bad at that time...if you didn't have to live in New York City!

WORLD MUSIC

If you're a music fan, then you're probably familiar with "world music" or at least the term. Even if you're not, you've probably at least heard the term at some point. If you were to ask someone, even a hardcore music lover, to define "world music" though, you'd probably get as many definitions as people!

So, what is world music and how has it influenced modern world pop culture?

To define the term, it probably helps to go back to when it was first coined. University of Connecticut music professor Robert E. Brown first used the term in the 1960s to describe different styles of traditionally non-Western music that were making their way into the West at the time. As time went on and technology got better, more and more non-Western styles became available in the West to the point that "world" became a category of its own.

Traditional music styles from Africa, Asia, Latin America, the Middle East, and Oceania—along with indigenous American and Australian music—are considered world music. With that said, there is no single definition of world music, so sometimes European traditional folk music, done with modern instruments, is considered world music.

As world music became more popular in the 1980s, different sub-genres formed including world beat, Afro-Cuban, Salsa, and different fusions. Combining different forms and styles of world music, as well as using obscure instruments, is part of the more recent trend in world music.

Random Facts:

- The world beat sub-genre became popular in the 1980s when musicians blended standard pop with non-Western music. One of the first mainstream bands to make this style popular was the American New Wave band, The Talking Heads.
- "Roots music" is the term often used in world music circles for music that is—or incorporates—folk music. Irish folk music is among the most popular European styles of folk music, made famous by bands such as The Pogues.
- The Irish musician Enya Patricia Brennan, better known by her mononym "Enya," is Ireland's best-selling solo musician and one of the most-recognized world music figures in the West.
- The didgeridoo is a wooden wind instrument that the Australian indigenous peoples have used for thousands of years. Several world and rock bands have used didgeridoos in their music, with one of the more notable examples being the Australian rock band Midnight Oil.
- Black South African Miriam Makeba was one of the first true world artists to have a crossover hit in America. Her 1964 album on the RCA label, *The World of Miriam Makeba* reached #86 on the Billboard 200.
- Googoosh has been a musician for more than 60 years and is the most popular Persian singer of all-time. Despite being sidelined by the Iranian government after the 1979 Islamic Revolution, her world popularity only seemed to grow. She is a polyglot who has recorded songs in several different languages and was finally allowed to leave Iran to tour for the first time in 2000.
- Traditional Nordic folk music and the music of the indigenous Sami people of Scandinavia are both considered world music and are quite popular throughout the world. Some European heavy

metal bands, such as Finntroll, incorporate Nordic and Sami folk elements into their acts and are therefore considered world music.

- The best-selling domestic musician in Brazil is also a priest! Father Marcelo Rossi has sold 3,328,468 copies of his 1998 album *Músicas para Louvar ao Senhor* to place him first among his countrymen and women in domestic sales.
- Immigration has played a major role in the rise in popularity of world music. Paris was once the epicenter of world music, hosting many bands and artists from its former African colonies, but later London and New York also became world music meccas.
- Qawwali is a form of traditional Islamic singing performed by Sufis. Nusrat Fateh Ali Khan is a notable Qawwali performer who collaborated with British musician Peter Gabriel.
- Nike Ardilla (1975-1995) is the best-selling musician in Indonesian history. She holds the #1 and #2 spots for record sales in Indonesia.
- The dizi is a bamboo flute that has been played in China for thousands of years. If you've ever seen the *Kill Bill* movies or the 1970s television show *Kung Fu*, then you've heard the dizi.
- Lebanese popstar Haifa Wehbe has been dazzling audiences for more than 15 years with her beautiful looks and voice. Wehbe's musical style is dance-pop with a heavy Middle Eastern influence, using traditional instruments such as the qanun and saz.
- Mongolians perform a very distinct form of traditional singing where multiple singers sing over each other. It is known as "Tuvan throat singing" because, to do it successfully, one has to sing from deep in the throat.
- Jazz fusion is a style that combines jazz with electric instruments, while "world fusion jazz" is a style that combines elements of Western jazz and any number of world music styles.

- One of the more unique blends in world music comes from the band Country for Syria. The band, whose members are from all over the world, combine traditional Middle Eastern music with American Country music, which is itself based on folk music.
- K-pop is generally not considered world music, but some K-pop stars, such as Sunmi, have incorporated traditional Korean instruments into their acts, so some would say that it is—or employs elements of—world music.
- The Chakachas, or Los Chakachas, was an early world music band. Although they were from Belgium, as the name indicates, the Chakachas were known for playing Caribbean and Latin style music. Although they had hits in Europe in the late 1950s and '60s, they are best remembered in the United States for their 1971 "Jungle Fever," which reached #8 on the Billboard Hot 100.
- "Township music" is a style of music that became popular in South Africa in the 1920s. It mixed Western jazz and Western instruments with the musical styles and instruments of southern Africa.
- The sitar is a traditional stringed instrument of South Asia that is often used on Indian influenced and based world music albums. It became more widely known in the West when The Beatles and other rock bands used it in some of their songs.

STAND UP AND TELL SOME JOKES

They say that comedy is the best medicine. If you've ever really been down and found yourself laughing at something genuinely funny, then you know that's true. The science behind the positive health benefits of humor and comedy is undeniable, which is why many of us turn to comedy when we need a little brightness in our lives.

Some of us may stream a comedy film while others turn to stand-up comedy. Most of us have watched at least a little stand-up comedy and many of us have favorite stand-ups. Richard Pryor, George Carlin, Janeane Garofalo, Chris Rock, Bill Hicks, and countless others have stood up on stage and delivered routines that have brought the house down. These have now been immortalized thanks to DVDs, YouTube, and other streaming services.

The origins of stand-up comedy can be traced back to several different sources in the late 1800s in the United States and Europe. Vaudeville acts usually featured plenty of comedy and occasionally acts that almost entirely consisted of jokes being told by a performer.

After World War II, stand-up comedy was a full-fledged nightclub genre of its own, with several different "circuits" and sub-genres, including some of the following: blue comedy, observational comedy, dark comedy, and prop comedy.

And as stand-up comedy became more widespread and lucrative, the acts became more complex. Many good comedians are also good writers. A good act, or "set," is written with an intro with multiple "bits" that follow a logical path or storyline.

A good comedian also comes prepared in the event they "bomb" or are faced with "hecklers." If those problems happen, the comedian reverts from their live patter to prewritten jokes to deal with a rough crowd.

The life of a stand-up comedian can be difficult, but the possibility of that big payoff at the end of the rainbow keeps millions trying it every year.

Random Facts:

- As you probably know, a heckler is a person who attempts to disrupt a comedian's performance. It's believed the term originated in the mid-1400s in England to refer to someone in the textile trade, but by the late 1800s it came to mean one "who harasses."
- Loretta Mary Aiken (1894-1975), better known as "Moms Mabley", was one of America's early stand-up comedians and a true pioneer. She didn't let being a Black woman deter her from touring the country and eventually becoming one of the country's best-known comics by the 1960s.
- In the early 1900s, British stand-up comedians were known as "front-cloth comics."
- "Blue comedy" or "blue acts" refers to comedians who focus on sexually explicit material. The origin of the term can be traced back to the late 1800s when "blue" was used as an adjective to describe bawdy and lewd speech and topics.
- Being a "joke thief" is about the worse thing a comedian can be accused of by their peers. Many notable stand-up comedians have been accused of plagiarizing others' works, but perhaps the most famous is the claim that Dennis Leary stole much of his material from the late Bill Hicks (1961-1994).
- Jerry Seinfeld is the world's wealthiest comedian, worth over $900 million. You probably know of him from his 1990s show *Seinfeld*, but as the show indicates, he got his start in stand-up.
- "Xiansheng" is a traditional form of Chinese stand-up comedy. It generally involves two performers who rapidly fire jokes and puns back and forth at each other.
- Observational comedy is a style of stand-up comedy that involves

the comedian talking about politics, current events, and/or pop culture humorously and cleverly. George Carlin (1937-2008) was one of the more notable observational comics.

- Red Foxx (1922-1991) was a well-known American comedian and actor who employed the African-American wordplay known as "the Dozens" into his brand of blue comedy. The Dozens involves clever putdowns and one-upmanship, which can be seen on Foxx's hit 1970s television show, *Sanford and Son*.
- As the name indicates, prop comedy is a style that involves the comedian using props and physical comedy for laughs. The American comedian Gallagher made prop comedy popular during the 1980s when he smashed watermelons during his act. After he became famous, fans began going to his shows with umbrellas and wearing raincoats.
- Some consider Mark Twain/Samuel Clemmons (1835-1910) as the father of American stand-up comedy. Although Twain is best known for his novels, such as *Tom Sawyer* and *Huck Finn*, he also gave live monologues that were known for their acerbic wit.
- Since many of the first American stand-up comics were Jewish, a stand-up comedy circuit developed in the Catskill Mountain resorts of upstate New York, also known as the "Jewish Alps" or the "Borscht Belt" from the 1920s to the '60s. George Burns, Woody Allen, and Mel Brooks all did shows in the Jewish Alps early in their careers.
- As with actors and musicians, most stand-up comedians work day jobs and pursue their passion at night for years. A gig on a comedy circuit can pay up to $100,000 while landing a five-minute set on a late-night talk show can net a comic a cool $2,000.
- "Clean comedy" is a comedy style that is essentially the opposite of blue comedy, with many of the comedians being practicing Christians. Many mainstream comedians have performed on the

growing Christian comedy circuit, including *Saturday Night Live* alumni Victoria Jackson, Sinbad, and the late Tim Conway.

- Every successful stand-up comic has "bombed" at least once in their career. It is estimated that nine out of ten jokes fail, so to make up for that, a successful comedian has to improvise and work the crowd.
- Max Miller (1894-1963) was considered by many to be the father of British stand-up comedy. Miller was known for his sarcasm and borderline blue jokes, which often got him censored and earned him the nickname "The Cheeky Chappie."
- Nightclubs dedicated specifically to stand-up comedy became popular in the 1980s. The two most important comedy nightclub chains are the Improv and the Laugh Factory.
- Although Jerry Seinfeld may be the comic with the most overall money, Kevin Hart made more money than any other comic in 2019 with $59 million!
- "Tight five" is a term used by stand-up comedians to refer to their best material that can be told in five minutes or less.
- British stand-up comedian Peter Kay holds the *Guinness World Record* for most successful comedy tour of all time for his 2010-2011 tour that sold more than 1.2 million tickets.

WHY IS IT "TOP 40"?

As we've talked about music topics in our *Big Book of Music Trivia*, the phrases "music charts" and "Top 40" have been mentioned a few times. This may seem pretty straightforward: it just refers to a list of the top 40 music hits in the country at the time, right?

Well, that would only be part of the answer.

The "Top 40" idea started when Omaha radio DJ, Todd Storz, compiled lists of the most popular jukebox songs in the area in the 1950s. He would then play those songs on a weekly broadcast, which became the basis for the later "Top 40" list. But there was one major feature absent from Storz's early lists—they didn't specify a number.

The idea of specifically 40 hits didn't become a common concept until the 1960s, and even then, there wasn't a consensus as to what it should sound like. The first true "Top 40" show to hit the radio waves was *American Top 40 (AT40)* hosted by Casey Kasem in 1970. Kasem, and now Ryan Seacrest, played the Top 40 songs, which were compiled from the *Billboard* Hot 100 chart.

The *Billboard* chart, which is considered the gold standard of charts in the American music industry, is formulated based on a combination of sales, radio play, and online streaming plays. As *Billboard's* compilation methods became more refined and based on 21st-century technology, *AT40* switched to a metric that used radio airplay for criteria for inclusion on its list and now uses charts created by the company Mediabase.

So, as it stands now, the United States has two primary lists that determine the top 40 hit songs in the country.

Random Facts:

- The *Billboard* Hot 100 chart is named for *Billboard* magazine, which began in 1894 as a trade magazine for bill posters. *Billboard* began covering silent film in the early 1900s and by the 1920s, with the growing influence of radio, it focused on music. It began compiling charts in the 1940s.
- Casey Kasem began broadcasting *AT40* on July 3, 1970, from radio station KDEO in El Cajon, California.
- The first number-one song on the *Billboard* Hot 100 was Ricky Nelson's "Poor Little Fool." The chart was released on August 4, 1958.
- A one-hit-wonder is generally considered to be an artist or band that charts with one hit and then is never heard from again. According to VH1's 2002 "10 Greatest One-Hit Wonders" chart, the 1996 hit "Macarena" by Los del Rio is the best one-hit-wonder ever.
- Most Top 40 charts, no matter the genre or country, are compiled weekly and often have a year-end list as well.
- Todd Storz would use the success of his radio format to build a media empire, but he died in 1964 of heart disease at the age of 39.
- Kasem hosted *AT40* from its inception in 1970 until 1998, and then again from 1998 to 2004. Shadoe Stevens hosted from 1988 to 1995 and Ryan Seacrest has been hosting the show since 2004.
- Before the *Billboard* Hot 100 chart debuted on August 4, 1958, *Billboard* listed the following three music charts: *Best Sellers in Stores, Most Played by Jockeys*, and *Most Played in Jukeboxes*.
- The *Billboard* Hot 100 chart was exclusively a "singles" chart until December 5, 1998. The nature of the record and radio business until that time favored such a chart as "singles" were sold as

45rpm/7″ vinyl singles in addition to full-length LPs. After several songs dominated the *Hot 100 Airplay* chart, which is based solely on radio plays, the Hot 100 moved to change from a "singles" to a "song" chart.

- When Kasem left *AT40* the first time, he started *Casey's Top 40* on the Westwood One radio network. The show aired from January 21, 1989 to March 21, 1998.
- "Hot Country Songs" is *Billboard's* country music chart. The 50-position chart comprises a combination of radio play, digital sales, and streaming.
- The Nielsen Broadcast Data System (BDS) is best known for tracking consumers' television-watching habits in the United States, Canada, and Mexico, but it's also used to track radio preferences.
- In 1983, comedian Rick Dees began his own top 40 radio show, *Rick Dees Weekly Top 40*. The show, which airs on more than 200 radio stations worldwide, relies on Dees' signature brand of humor that includes plenty of impressions.
- Mariah Carey and R&B group Boyz II Men have the record for the longest time at #1 on the *Billboard* Top 100 with their hit "One Sweet Day." It was #1 for 16 weeks in 1995 and 1996.
- *Billboard* also has another Top 40 list known as the "Mainstream Top 40." The list is compiled based on radio airplay, so other songs that sell well digitally are not considered. Swedish dance/pop band Ace of Base holds the record for the longest time at #1 on the Mainstream Top 40. Their song "I Saw the Sign" was #1 for 14 weeks in 1994.
- The chart year for *Billboard* is from the first week of December to the final week of November. That means your favorite Christmas releases are included in the following year's statistics.
- Although the *Billboard* charts—and top 40 charts in general—are

often derided by fans and musicians of styles considered "underground" or non-mainstream, many metal, alternative, and even punk fans have created their own top 40 charts on the Internet.

- *Country Countdown USA* is the country music answer to *AT40*. It's a radio show nationally syndicated by the Westwood One network that counts down the top 30 current hits in country music. The show uses a similar metric as *AT40* does to compile its list.
- Many other countries also have their own top 40 lists. For instance, Mexican Airplay is a top 40 chart compiled by *Billboard* of singles that receive airplay on Mexican radio stations.
- Maverick American millionaire Gordon McLendon introduced the Storz top 40 concept to a wider number of radio stations across the United States in the 1960s.

TELENOVELAS

People all over the world have different ways to escape the hectic and stressful world of everyday life. Reality television has become one of the primary forms of entertainment escapism over the last 20 years, providing hours of entertainment for consumers at an affordable price for the production companies.

Before reality television was the rage, soap operas were one of the most common forms of escapism in the United States. Soap operas are daily, serialized dramas that focus on the glamorous, criminal, and often improbable lives of a variety of characters. Because they use a winning formula, soap operas are still fairly popular.

If you go south of the border, though, there is a style of soap opera that even reality television can't beat. I'm talking about telenovelas. The most basic definition of a telenovela is a Spanish-language soap opera that is popular in Latin America. There are some other notable differences between it and its north of the border counterpart.

An American soap opera can run for several years, or even decades, before being canceled. They are written with no particular end date in mind. On the other hand, Latin American telenovelas are conceived with a very definite run in mind, which can be deduced from the term itself: telenovela is a combination of "television" and "novel," and novels always have a definite ending.

Mexico is the epicenter of Latin American telenovela production, so actors from across the Spanish-speaking world often go there to add to their resumes.

Random Facts:

- Most telenovelas only run for about a year or less. Every telenovela has a conclusion and resolution, usually with the protagonist overcoming obstacles and getting their love interest and with the antagonist getting their just dues.
- Actress Selma Hayek got her big break in the 1988 Mexican telenovela, *Un Nuevo Amanecer*.
- Although Mexico may be the telenovela capital, the first telenovela was a 1951 Portuguese-language show from Brazil called *Sua vida me pertence*.
- The first telenovela produced in Mexico was *Senda prohibida* in 1957-58.
- Like American soap operas, telenovelas are broadcast five or even six days a week, but they are usually shown in the evenings.
- Telenovelas were initially popular in Cuba, but the communist revolution that put Castro in power in 1958 changed things. Many of the Cuban telenovela writers were exiled, with several ending up in Mexico where they began writing new series.
- Most telenovelas are set in middle or working-class neighborhoods and centered on the trials and tribulations of Latin Americans of those classes. Some telenovelas, though, incorporate elements of mystery, science fiction, and horror. Another subgenre that is growing in popularity, especially in Mexico, is narco-themed telenovelas.
- A version of telenovels called "sinetrons" is popular in Indonesia. Like telenovelas, Sinetrons are aired daily and usually last for about five months.
- A 1998 study found that 53% of 12- to 62-year-olds in Latin America watch telenovelas regularly, although the percentages

vary widely from country to country. Brazil was number one in the survey with 73% of the people in that demographic watching telenovelas regularly, while the Dominican Republic was last with 26%. Perhaps somewhat surprising, only 34% of Mexicans in that age group claim to have watched telenovelas regularly.

- One of the most popular telenovelas of all time around the world is the 1979 Mexican production *Los ricos también lloran* (*The Rich Cry Too*). After already having been very popular in Latin America, the show was played in the Soviet Union in 1991.
- The American sit-coms *Ugly Betty* and *Jane the Virgin* were based on Colombian and Venezuelan telenovelas, respectively, but they were adapted into a more traditional American-style weekly format.
- American actor Erik Estrada is best known for playing officer Frank "Ponch" Poncharello on the hit show *CHiPs* in the 1970s and '80s, but he also starred in a Mexican telenovela later in his career. Estrada played the lead role in *Dos Mujeres, un Camino* in 1993-4.
- According to the British Broadcasting Company, hundreds of millions of people watch telenovelas every day, with some estimating that the number could be as high as two billion.
- A 2012 report states that 5.6 million people in the United States watched telenovelas regularly versus only 2.9 million for traditional soap operas.
- Telemundo was the first television channel broadcasting telenovelas, and Univision soon followed in the 1990s. Between: 1990 - 2015 these two companies made over 121 telenovelas for distribution.
- It is estimated that about 3,000 hours of telenovelas are produced in Mexico every year at a cost of around $250 million. Mexico has produced over 110 novelas between 2010- 2019.

- Telemundo and Univision are American based television networks that show telenovelas. The majority of Telemundo's programming is first-run telenovelas produced by the network. The majority of Univision's programming is also telenovelas, although they are produced by other networks.
- Brazilian telenovelas are not shy about showing some skin. Female nudity is not uncommon in Brazilian telenovelas. This, combined with the shows being in Portuguese, means they are among the least imported shows in other countries. Many Brazilian telenovelas have to be heavily edited or shown late at night in other countries.
- Germany got into the telenovela craze in the 2000s. German telenovelas tend to be love stories without the action of Latin American telenovelas.
- *Corazón salvaje* is the title of four different Mexican telenovelas. All four series—1966, 1977, 1993, and 2009—were based on a 1957 historical fiction novel of the same name by Caridad Bravo Adams.
- *El Señor de los Cielos,* was the most expensive telenovela ever produced by Telemundo, although some would argue it's not a true telenovela. Although *El Señor* is aired daily and follows the typical conventions of a telenovela, it has now aired for seven full seasons (April 15, 2013—January 31, 2020).

GONE COUNTRY

Many different popular musical styles have been spawned on American soil. Among them are blues, rock n' roll, bluegrass, and country and western. Country and western music, often just abbreviated as "country," is perhaps the most "American" of all the styles, drawing inspiration from all corners of American society to create a sound that has several sub-genres.

Today, country music is one of the most popular musical styles in America, the most popular style with older Americans, and it has been exported to and is popular in several other countries throughout the world.

Country music is quite popular in Canada and some of country music's earliest and most influential crooners, such as Hank Snow, were born in Canada.

Perhaps owing to the similar gaucho culture in Latin America, country is also popular south of the border and it has been modified in many Latin American countries to fit their unique musical tastes.

Country music is also popular in parts of Europe and Asia and is a popular style in Australia. Did you know that Olivia Newton-John is Australian?

Country music began in 1920s in the Appalachia Mountains when mountain folk began strumming Celtic folk songs with new instruments, such as the banjo, with lyrics and rhythm that embodied their experience in America. Over time, the Appalachian style mixed with the cowboy ballads of the Western United States grew to form what we would call country music by the 1930s and '40s.

The 1950s brought the influence of rock, blues, and gospel into country, which was personified by Elvis Presley, and by the 1960s country music was a multi-million dollar industry based in Nashville.

Today, country music continues to be big business economically and is one of the driving forces of pop culture in the United States and beyond.

Random Facts:

- Johnny Cash's (1932-2003) "I Walk the Line" was number one on the *Billboard* country chart for 43 weeks in 1956-1957 and entered the *Billboard* 100 at #20.
- Drums were generally eschewed in the early years of country music. Bob Wills and the Texas Playboys are believed to have been the first act to use a drummer on the stage of the Grand Ole Opry in December 1944.
- "Honky-tonk" is a strange and uniquely American term that has its origins in country music. Honky-tonk can refer to a bar that plays live country music, it can be used as a verb to go to such a bar, or—most commonly—it refers to a subgenre of country that came out of Texas in the 1950s.
- Before Nashville was the country capital, Atlanta was the heart of the scene in the 1920s and '30s.
- Shania Twain's 1997 *Come on Over* is the best-selling studio country album of all time. It has sold over 40 million copies, which means it has gone platinum 20 times. It is the eighth best-selling album in American history. Not bad for a Canadian country girl!
- Music historians believe Henry Gilliland and Eck Robertson recorded the first commercially based country song on June 30, 1922. The songs they recorded together were "Arkansas Traveler" and "Turkey in the Straw."
- Country music in general sells moderately well across Latin America, but it does best in Mexico.
- "Bro-country" is a subgenre of country music that became popular in the 2010s. The music is influenced by 21st-century hip hop, hard rock and electronica.. The lyrics focus primarily on attractive young women, the consumption of alcohol, partying, and pickup trucks.

- Tex Ritter (1905-1975) was influential in country music's early years in the 1920s and '30s, helping to bring the style to a wider audience. He was also one of the first country music stars to act in movies and was the father of late actor John Ritter (1948-2003), who is best known for his role as "Jack Tripper" on the 1970s-'80s sitcom, *Three's Company*.
- Marie Osmund became the youngest musician to reach #1 on the *Billboard* country chart in 1973 at the age of 14 with her hit, "Paper Roses."
- The style of country known as the "Bakersfield sound" developed in Bakersfield, California by 1930s Dustbowl transplants from Oklahoma. Merle Haggard and Buck Owens were two of the best-known and most popular Bakersfield sound musicians.
- In Canada, country music is most popular in the prairie provinces, which are geographically close to the American Western states and also share similarities to the Midwest and Southern states.
- Tex Morton (1916-1983) was one of the most important musicians in early Australian country music. Morton picked up the name while touring in the United States and Canada in the 1950s and always sang with an American accent. Despite being a legend of Australian country music, Morton was actually from New Zealand!
- "Outlaw" country refers to a subgenre of country music that became popular in the late 1960- 1980's. It was heavily influenced by the honky-tonk style, but with lyrics and attitude that were indicative of the counter-culture of the era.
- Although her more recent stuff is not considered "true country" by hardcore country music fans, Taylor Swift is the best-selling country music artist of all time with more than 121 million certified album sales.
- If you only consider more purely country artists, then Garth

Brooks is the biggest seller with more than 137million certified albums sold.

- Country music has found its way to some interesting places. Bobby Cash, born Bal Kishore Das Loiwal, was born and raised in India, but he acquired a love of country music from his aunt who lived in Nashville. Cash is the biggest country star in India, but he has also charted hits in Australia.
- Owing to Australia's similar Celtic ethnic background to Appalachia, and how its vast Outback compares to the American West, Australian country music developed on its own, yet was also influenced by American country. One of the early influences on Australian country were "bush ballads," which were songs sung by farmers and workers in the Outback.
- Despite being more conservative, and sometimes because of it, some country music acts have been the subject of controversy. Most recently, Georgia band Confederate Railroad has had some of their bookings cancelled due to their name and the use of Confederate flags in the band's logo.
- Although the early country music recording studios were in Atlanta and they later moved to Nashville, Bristol, Tennessee has been officially recognized as the "Birthplace of Country Music" by the United States Congress. The city acquired that moniker because it was the site of the "Bristol sessions" in 1927, which were a series of recordings that led to the birth of the actual industry.

CHAPTER 3:

Sports and Leisure

MOST PEOPLE CALL IT FOOTBALL

The most popular sport in the world by far—in terms of the number of fans, players, and revenue—is football, or as it is known in the United States, Canada, and Australia, soccer. The sport of football includes hundreds of leagues of various levels, men and women, playing in nearly every country on the planet. Football has brought countries and people together during tournaments and championships, but it has also been a source of violence.

But you're not necessarily wrong if you do refer to it as soccer.

You see, the proper name for football/soccer is actually "association football," which officially began when the rules were codified in England in 1863 by the Football Association of England. Shortly after being given that name, many people began shortening "association" to "socc" and adding "er" on as a reference to those who play the sport.

An international governing body was created in 1904 in Paris, France. Known as the International Federation of Association Football (FIFA), it standardized the rules and oversees play. The most basic rules of 11 players to a side/team and the size of the field/pitch had already been established, but FIFA fleshed out some of the more nuanced details of the game, including yellow and red cards, time limits, extra time, and more.

Today, association football is the highest-grossing sport in the world, worth billions of dollars with multi-millionaire players who travel from continent to continent, building their brands along the way.

Random Facts:

- There are several different versions of sports that people know as football: Australian rules football, rugby union, rugby league, Gaelic football, and gridiron (American football). All games that are called "football" have similar British origins and are often known as "football codes."
- The five biggest association football leagues in terms of revenue and sales are all in Europe: the English Premier League, the German Bundesliga, Serie A in Italy, La Liga in Spain, and Ligue 1 in France.
- The FIFA World Cup is held every four years to determine the best national men's team in the world. A player may play for a club team in one country but play for the team of his nationality or citizenship in the World Cup. The tournament begins with the teams playing in a regional qualifying stage that is then reduced to a 32-team field that most people consider the "World Cup."
- The goalkeeper is the only player allowed to touch the ball with their hands in association football.
- An association football game officially lasts for 90 minutes divided into two 45 minute halves. Unlike most other team sports, the clock in association football begins at zero and counts to 45 minutes instead of beginning at 45 minutes and counting down.
- You've probably heard of retired Brazilian footballer Edson Arantes do Nascimento by his more common nickname, Pelé. Nascimento, who is considered to be the greatest player in a country full of great players, claimed in his autobiography that he doesn't know the origin of the nickname.
- The Union of European Football Associations (UEFA) is an organization that conducts an annual tournament of the best men's club teams in Europe, known as the UEFA or European

Cup. The teams qualify by playing in their normal leagues and then advance to a 32-team final group.

- The 2014 World Cup hosted by Brazil is believed to have been the most attended World Cup with a total attendance of 3.4 million people
- Although all European leagues draw the top talent from around the world, the English Premier Leagues is the best and generates the most revenue with nearly $6 billion in 2019-2020, which is about two billion more than the leagues in Spain and Germany.
- Association football is often given the moniker "the beautiful game." Although Pelé popularized that term in the 1960s, it was around before that time.
- As of 16 July 2020, Real Madrid have won a record 34 La Liga and a record 13 European Cup / UEFA Champions League trophies
- Women's association football follows the same rules as the men and has been played since the late 1800s, but it wasn't organized into leagues until after World War II. Although association football in general lags behind gridiron football, baseball, basketball, and even hockey in popularity in the United States, the American women's association football team has been successful, winning four FIFA World Cups.
- Brazil is the most successful national team in men's association football, having won five FIFA World Cups: 1958, 1962, 1970, 1994, 2002.
- Josef Bican -Josef "Pepi" Bican (25 September 1913 – 12 December 2001) was a Czech-Austrian professional footballer who played as a striker. He is the most prolific goal scorer of all time in league matches, first level championships matches, official matches and total matches (considering only players who mostly played at the highest level and taking into account goals scored in official matches played .

- One of the rule features that draws fans to association football is the fact that gameplay rarely stops. There are no timeouts, but stoppages of time for injuries, substitutions, and the playing ball going out of bounds are recorded by the referee. The "stoppage time" is tabulated at the end of the match and added to the overall time of the match.
- Ties (equal scores for each team) are common in association football and usually help a team in the overall standings. In cases where a definite winner needs to be determined, such as in a tournament, "penalty shootouts" are used.
- The inaugural FIFA Women's World Cup was held in China in 1991. The United States was the champion.
- When giving a player a foul, the referee holds up a yellow card or red card. A red card means a player is ejected from the game and two yellow cards in a game equals a red card. If a player is dismissed, the team cannot substitute a new player, meaning that a penalized team has to play with one less player on the pitch.
- Although all sports have rowdy fans, association football is known for hooliganism that is sometimes quite organized. The worst hooligan violence happened on May 25, 1985 in Heysel Stadium in Brussels, Belgium when Liverpool FC hooligans stormed Juventas fans, causing a wall collapse that killed 39 people in the process.
- The qualifying regions for the FIFA World Cup are not given equal consideration. FIFA decides the number of teams each region will send to the finals based on the overall strength of the teams in those regions. For instance, Europe has 55 teams and sent 14 teams to the finals in 2018, while Asia has 47 teams but only five qualified to make it to Russia.

SOME COUNTRIES HAVE A VERSION OF FOOTBALL OF THEIR OWN

As mentioned previously, there are several "football codes" or different styles of the game throughout the world. The countries where these other styles of football are more popular—the United States, Canada, Australia, and Ireland, to a certain extent—usually call their national brand "football" and association football "soccer."

Let's start with "gridiron."

Gridiron is a football code known simply as "football" in the United States and Canada. Although it's more commonly associated with the United States because the largest and most popular gridiron league, the National Football League (NFL), is based in the United States, it evolved in the 1800s from a combination of soccer and rugby. Plus it has a definite Canadian influence.

The rules of gridiron football were first developed at McGill University in Montreal, Quebec and then sent to clubs around Canada and eventually exported to the United States in the late 1800s.

Although there are some minor differences between the Canadian and American styles of gridiron, they both are played on a field (100 yards in the U.S. or 110 yards in Canada) with goalposts at either end. The field is divided by "yard markers" that give the field a gridiron look. The gameplay most closely resembles rugby.

Two other football codes that also evolved from and resemble rugby, even more so than gridiron, are Australian rules football and Gaelic football. Although Australian Rules football may resemble rugby at first glance, it has several notable differences, namely that the ball can be advanced through kicks and "hand passes" in any direction and all scoring is done by kicking the ball through goal posts. There are four goal posts with the middle two posts nominated as the highest scoring area.

Gaelic football is a rugby-influenced code that was first standardized in the late 1800s in Ireland. Although some of the scoring and gameplay is a bit different than Australian football, the two codes are similar enough that international hybrid-rules games between the best Gaelic and Australian players have been held since the late 1960s.

Random Facts:

- The United States, Canada, and Australia all have professional football leagues. Although Gaelic football has leagues, they are all amateur. Since the codes are similar, in recent years some of the top Gaelic football players have been drafted into the Australian Football League (AFL).
- In Canadian football, there are 12 players on the field at a time, while in American football there are 11.
- The proper Gaelic word for Gaelic football is *Peil Ghaelach*.
- Various forms of football, known as *caid*, were played in Ireland for centuries, but it was rugby's influence that led to the codification of Gaelic football. Leagues were officially formed on the Emerald Isle in 1887.
- Australian Rules football is played on an oval field that is 150 to 200 yards in length. Gaelic football fields are rectangular and 142 to 160 yards in length.
- Cricket fields often double for football fields in Australia, while Gaelic football is often played on rugby fields in Ireland.
- There are 18 players on the field per team in men's Australian Rules football, but only 15 in Gaelic football.
- The major football league in Canada is the Canadian Football League (CFL). It was founded in 1958 and is considered the second-best league after the NFL in terms of quality and revenue. The difference in overall revenue, though, is quite large, with the NFL bringing in about $14 billion per year, dwarfing the CFL's still respectable $200 million.
- There is no offside rule in Australian or Gaelic football.
- The rules of Australian Rules football were codified in the 1850s.

The VFL (now AFL) formed in 1896 and has 18 men's teams. It is the most-watched and highest revenue-generating team sport in Australia.

- Several leagues have tried to challenge the NFL hegemony in the United States since World War II. The American Football League (1960-1970), the World Football League (1974-1975), and the United States Football League (1982-1986). All three leagues folded, although the AFL became part of the NFL in 1970.
- Irishman Tadgh Kennelly is one of the most successful athletes to have played both Gaelic and Australian football. After playing in the lower Gaelic leagues for a few years, he was signed by the Sydney Swans of the AFL and played for many years in the league. He also played Gaelic football in the AFL offseason and is the only athlete to have won a championship in the top leagues in both football codes.
- An Australian Rules football game consists of four 20-minute quarters. Unlike soccer, the clock is stopped for injuries and the ball going out of bounds.
- There are nine teams in the Canadian Football League divided into two divisions. All teams take part in a playoff where the trophy is the Grey Cup.
- A Gaelic football goalpost looks very similar to a rugby or gridiron goalpost. One point is scored if a player kicks or "fists" the bar over the crossbar and three if the player can get it under the crossbar.
- Australian Rules goalposts are the most unique looking of all the football codes. There are two inner posts and two shorter, outer posts. A player scores six points by kicking the ball between the two inner posts and one point for putting it between the outer posts.
- Tackling the ball carrier is a major part of gameplay in all four

football codes.

- In Canadian and American football, the team with the ball has to generally gain ten yards, barring penalties, to get a new set of "downs" or tries. In Canadian football, a team gets three downs before they have to "punt" the ball or turn it over on downs to the other team. In American football, though, the team with the ball gets four downs.
- All four football codes use different balls. American and Canadian football use types of spherical-shaped balls that are almost indistinguishable. Australian Rules football uses an oval-shaped football, with more rounded tips than American and Canadian footballs. Gaelic football uses a round spherical ball that more closely resembles a volleyball.
- Both Australian and Gaelic football players are able to pass the ball forward with a closed fist strike (handball or handpass) or a kick, as the play is moving downfield. In Canadian and American football, the ball can only be passed forward from behind the line of scrimmage (where the play starts).

THE DRINKING MAN'S SPORT

Beer and sports, no matter the sport and no matter the country, seem to go well together, almost as if God intended it to be that way. What more fun is there than sitting around a television with some friends and family watching your favorite team play your favorite sport?

Or better yet, what beats drinking a tall frosty one on a warm day at a packed stadium? Yes, beer and sports seem to be a match made in heaven, but if there is one sport that is more beercentric than others it has to be baseball.

One of the most interesting aspects of baseball and beer is that copious amounts of alcohol never seemed to have slowed down the best baseball players of all time.

Babe Ruth, who is still considered by many to be the best baseball player of all time, shattered records on the field, won numerous batting titles, became the first player to hit 500 home runs, and was the American League home-run champion 12 times. He was also a good pitcher, compiling a 94-46 record as a pitcher, a lifetime 2.28 ERA.

Ruth's incredible statistics are bolstered by the fact that he was often drunk or hungover when he had some of his biggest games!

But heavy drinking wasn't just the prerogative of early baseball players.

Boston Red Sox great Wade Boggs was known to pound beers just as hard and heavy as Ruth, even claiming after he retired that he once drank 107 beers in a day! None of that stopped the Hall of Famer from making 12 All-star appearances and becoming a member of the illustrious 3,000 hit club.

It almost seems like the power of beer helps some of these players!

Random Facts:

- For years there was a legend that Wade Boggs' drank 64 lite beers on a cross-country flight and then went 3 for 5 the next day at the plate against the Seattle Mariners. The legend was the subject of a 2015 episode of the sitcom *It's Always Sunny in Philadelphia.*
- In an era before refrigeration was common, Ruth would have the bathtubs of his hotel rooms filled with iced beer so that he had some to drink when he got back after hitting the nightclubs.
- Jeff Nelson, a former teammate of Boggs, claimed that it was normal for him to drink 50 or 60 beers in a single sitting.
- Another Babe Ruth story states one of his New York Yankees teammates found him drinking in a Philadelphia brothel with a woman on each knee. He was drinking heavily as the sex workers poured champagne on his head and rubbed it in like shampoo. He made it to the park the next day on a couple of hours of sleep and hit two home runs.
- New York Yankees great Mickey Mantle said he started his mornings with a big glass filled with at least one shot of Brandy, some Kahlua, and cream.
- Drinking and baseball are so synonymous that there is even a drinking game called "baseball." Baseball is best described as a hybrid of beer pong and flip cup, where the object is—you guessed it—to drink your opponents under the table.
- Supposedly, New York Yankees pitcher David Wells was "half-drunk" when he threw a perfect game against the Minnesota Twins on May 17, 1998.
- As more evidence of the link between beer and baseball, three stadiums are at least partially sponsored by breweries and have their companies in the names: Busch Stadium in St. Louis, Coors Field in Denver, and Miller Park in Milwaukee.

- The National League, which is the older of the two leagues in Major League Baseball, was started by teetotalers. Several teams were expelled or quit the league in the 1880s due to prohibitions on selling beer at the parks.
- Curt Welch (1862-1896) was one of the early greats of professional baseball and he was also a heavy drinker. Welch liked his beer so much that he kept some on ice behind a billboard in the outfield.
- Detroit Tigers first baseman Miguel Cabrera has been known to put down more than a few drinks. The night before a one-game playoff against the Minnesota Twins, he drank for several hours with friends, but unlike Boggs or Wells, he didn't play well the next day and his team lost.
- Longtime Chicago Cubs announcer Harry Caray was known for his loud and rambunctious style, which was probably due to him being drunk most of the time. Once while intoxicated, Caray hailed a cab but it was a Chicago Police car. Luckily, the cop gave Caray a ride to his destination. It's safe to say the officer wasn't a White Sox fan!
- Wrigley Field in Chicago is consistently the most expensive stadium for beer prices. If you want to drink a cold one and watch the Cubs live, you're looking at paying $9.50 for a single beer. At the other end of the spectrum, you're only looking at paying $4 per beer at Chase Field in Arizona.
- Fictional bar owner Sam Malone on the television series *Cheers* was a former Boston Red Sox pitcher who was known for being a womanizer and an alcoholic. The Sam Malone character made his first appearance on television in September 1982, just months after Boggs began playing for the Red Sox—coincidence?
- Of course, drinking and baseball don't always equal a good time. New York Mets pitcher Dwight Gooden struggled with alcohol and drug addiction his entire life. After the Mets won the World

Series in 1986, Gooden began drinking heavily and visited his drug dealer to buy some cocaine. He ended up missing the team's ceremonial victory parade through New York City.

- Due to his heavy partying ways, the New York Yankees made Babe Ruth sign a morals clause in 1922. It did little to slow him down.
- Rogers Browning was another early professional baseball player who may have gained strength from beer. He was said to rarely drink in the offseason but drank heavily from April to September.
- The Boston Red Sox were supposed to have a big year in 2011, but when they faded out during the final stretch run and didn't make the playoffs, everyone was looking for answers. Apparently, pitchers John Lester, Josh Beckett, and John Lackey spent a lot of time in the clubhouse drinking beer, playing video games, and eating chicken.
- According to one source, Mantle and Yankees manager Billy Martin once got so drunk together in Detroit that they thought it'd be a good idea to climb from the balcony of their room to the other players' rooms. They were on the 22nd floor.
- The American Association was an early professional baseball league that existed from 1882 to 1891. Although it played under most of the same rules as the National League, it allowed its players and fans to drink, earning it the nickname "the Beer and Whiskey League."

THOSE WHO RUN FAST

For most cultures throughout history, sports have been a pastime, a way to blow off some steam and maybe make a little money in the process. Professional athletes (or their equivalent) have existed since ancient times and there have always been people who have bet on sporting events.

Sports have also been a way for people to hone their bodies and to get into and stay in shape. We all know that exercise is good for the mind and body and that if you can find a sport or exercise you like, it just makes it that much easier.

But for some people exercise and sports isn't just something they do; it's who they are.

The Tarahumara people of the northern Mexican state of Chihuahua only number about 70,000 today and they generally keep themselves, isolated from greater Mexican society by staying in their small communities in the Sierra Madre Occidental Mountains. Many of us in the outside world don't know much about them. But they have an interesting story: they run for no other reason than to run.

The Tarahumara people's name in their language is Rarámuri, which means "those who run fast." And run fast and far they do, competing against each other and outsiders in ultra-marathons that can go more than 200 miles in rough mountain and canyon country. Incredibly, they often complete these runs in two days and do so wearing nothing but sandals.

They don't run for money or fame; they run because it's a part of who they are.

Random Facts:

- The Tarahumara people also live in the states of Chihuahua, Durango, and Sonora, although most are located in Chihuahua.
- The Rarámuri language is in the Uto-Aztecan family of languages. It is related to Nahuatl, which was the language of the Aztecs. There are actually several different dialects of Tarahumara which are so different from each other that it is difficult for speakers of one to understand speakers of the other.
- The running shoe of the Tarahumara is known as a *huarache*. It consists only of a sole that is held by straps. The Tarahumara people originally made the soles from leather but then later used the tread from car tires.
- The Tarahumara people are so isolated that it wasn't until 1889 when Americans began to learn of their existence. Frederick Schwatka led an exploration team through northern Mexico that year and later wrote about the tribe's existence.
- An "ultra-marathon" is considered any race that is longer than the standard 26.2-mile marathon, although most are a minimum of 30 miles, with the International Association of Athletics Federation (IAAF) keeping records of best times.
- Some Tarahumara people interpret Rarámuri to mean "runner with the ball," which may indicate some origin or affiliation with the Mesoamerican ball game.
- Some ultra-marathons are also timed events. The participants are to run a set amount of time ranging anywhere from six hours to six days, with the winner being the person who covers the most ground.
- Most of the Tarahumara races are held friendly competitions between villages and often during religious celebrations, such as the Feast of St. John.

- American Ted Corbitt (1919-2007) is often thought of as the "father of long-distance running" and one of the primary forces behind the emergence of competitive ultra-marathon running in the 1970s.
- Although the Tarahumara people usually keep their running events within their communities, they have occasionally ventured out to show their skills to the world. On March 21, 1925, six Tarahumara runners—three men and three women—left their community for the first time to run in an exhibition race in Texas. The men ran from San Antonia to Austin for a total of 82 miles, while the women ran a standard marathon.
- The record for the longest time in an ultra-marathon is held by Yiannis Kouros. He ran for six days in 2005 in Australia, covering 645 miles in the process, but New Zealand ultra-marathon runner Sandy Berwick was able to cover more miles, 548, when she broke the six-day women's record in 1990 in Australia.
- The Tarahumara people begin running at ten, but other genetic factors probably play a role in their running prowess. Dr. Dale Groom of the University of Oklahoma did a study of the people in the 1970s and found that the Tarahumara people rarely had heart or respiratory problems and deaths from those factors were virtually unknown. He concluded that genetics plays a large factor in their running success and health.
- As more knowledge of the Tarahumara has become known in the last two decades, huaraches have been manufactured by some companies. They are often made with pre-cut rubber soles and hemp straps.
- In addition to holding the six-day ultra-marathon record, Yiannis Kouros also holds the records for 100 kilometers, 1,000 miles, 24 hours, and 48 hours. Kouros' running prowess and Greek background have earned him the nickname the "Running God" and "Pheidippides' Successor." Pheidippides was the legendary

ancient Greek runner who ran from Athens to Sparta and back (150 miles) to request help against the Persian invasion in 490 BCE. He then ran to the battlefield near Marathon (25 miles) and back to Athens to announce the Greek victory before dying.

- Tarahumaras Jose Torres and Aurelio Terrazas competed in the marathon event in the 1928 Summer Olympics in Amsterdam, Netherlands, finishing 32nd and 35th.
- Another factor that seems to aid in the Tarahumaras' running success is the method with which they run. Instead of running on their toes, Tarahumara runners strike on their heels and push off from their mid-feet in short strides. The effect is that their feet barely leave the ground and the run looks more like a glide.
- In 1992, Rick Fisher, an American wilderness guide based in Tucson, Arizona, began sponsoring male and female Tarahumara runners in marathons in the United States.
- The 2009 book, *Born to Run: A Hidden Tribe, Superathletes, and the Greatest Race the World Has Never See* by Christopher McDougall chronicles the Tarahumara culture and their running abilities. It has sold more than three million copies, making it a best-seller.
- Style and genetics may have plenty to do with the Tarahumara running success, but diet and culture also play a role. The Tarahumara diet is high in carbs, consisting mainly of pinto bean and corn tortillas, which is a great way to get the energy needed for those long runs.
- The Tarahumara people are also extremely community orientated, which is for the most part in opposition to the very individually centric Western culture. Tarahumara runners use this communal philosophy when they run; always doing so as a team, pacing each other as they go.

WHY IS IT CALLED A PUCK?

Ice hockey, or simply known as "hockey" in the countries where it's popular and played, is the fifth-most popular team sport in the world and is the most popular cold-weather/winter sport.

Hockey is the most popular sport in Canada, is number one or two across many Eastern European and Scandinavian countries, and is number four overall in the United States, although higher in states like Minnesota, North Dakota, Michigan, some Western states, and parts of New England.

The National Hockey League (NHL) is hockey's premier professional league, but there are scores more minor leagues scattered throughout the world.

If you are a soccer fan but not familiar with hockey, you'll notice they have some similarities. You'll also notice that occasionally hockey has more in common with boxing or even a gang fight.

So, how did hockey originate and become a popular sport? And what exactly is a puck?

Hockey evolved out of a combination of polo, Irish hurling, and soccer, which were brought to Canada by British colonists. The word "puck" is derived from the Gaelic word *puc*, which is what the ball is called in hurling.

Because Canada is a cold place in the winter and its lakes and ponds freeze, people started playing hurling games on ice and eventually began wearing skates during the games. Organized hockey as we know it today began in Montreal where the first indoor game was played in 1875. The rules were codified shortly thereafter and by the early 1900s, the first professional leagues were in existence.

It took a while for hockey to spread, but by the mid-20th century, it was truly an international sport.

Random Facts:

- There are six players from each team on the "ice" at a time, not considering penalties: three forwards, two defensemen, and one goalie. Unlike soccer, teams are allowed unlimited substitutions in most hockey leagues and often do mass substitutions or "line changes."
- Hockey has similar offside rules as soccer.
- Penalized players are sent to the "penalty box" for "minor" penalties of two minutes or "major" penalties of five minutes. A team with one or more players in the box is said to be "shorthanded," while the team with the player(s) advantage is said to be on a "power play."
- A hockey field is called a "rink." The dimensions vary by league, but the NHL standard is 200 by 85 feet. The centerline is where the "face-off" starts the game by the referee dropping the puck. There are two "blue lines" that indicate when a player may potentially be offside. There are two face-off circles and the goal lines. The line between oval line in front of the goal is known as the "crease," which is essentially the goalie's protection zone.
- Goalies can be "pulled" in hockey leaving an "open net."
- Andy Brown was the NHL last goalie to play without a helmet on April 7, 1974.
- The "Original Six" NHL teams were the Boston Bruins, Chicago Black Hawks, Detroit Redwings, Montreal Canadians, Toronto Maple Leafs, and New York Rangers.
- "Junior hockey" is the highest form of amateur hockey leagues in Canada and the United States. The highest level leagues are governed by the Canadian Hockey League and United States Hockey League.

- Gerry Geran (1896-1981) was the first American born player to play in the NHL. He played in the late 1910s and 1920s.
- Although illegal, fighting is an important part of hockey. Players are given five-minute penalties for fighting and can be ejected, but coaches strategically use their best fighters, known as "enforcers" or "goons" to change the momentum of a game or to intimidate the other team's goal scorers.
- There is a difference in style between North American and European hockey. The European game relies more on finesse, while American and Canadian players like to "check" more and aren't afraid to "goon things up" on occasion.
- The Stanley Cup is the championship trophy awarded to the best NHL team every year. It was first awarded in 1893 and is named for Lord Stanley Preston, who was the Governor-General of Canada at the time.
- The Winter Olympics is now the showcase of the best hockey players in the world playing for their national teams, but it wasn't always this way. The Olympic committee didn't begin allowing professionals to play in the tournament until 1988 and the NHL didn't allow their players to do so until 1998. With that said, the Soviet Union's team was always comprised of what were essentially professionals, which is why they dominated the tournament for so many years.
- Wayne Gretzky is considered by most hockey fans to be the greatest player of all-time. Nicknamed the "Great One," the Hall of Famer held 61 NHL records when he retired in 1999 and is still the all-time goals leader with 894.
- Women's hockey started to become popular in the 1990s. There was enough interest from players and fans for the National Women's Hockey League to be formed in 2015.
- Although the American junior leagues are generally considered

inferior to those in Canada, National Collegiate Athletic Association Division I hockey is considered far better than the Canadian college system. Some schools, such as the University of Minnesota, consciously try to recruit the best local talent, but many Canadians and Europeans are attracted to NCAA programs to build their draft potential and to get a free education.

- The NHL draft is usually held every June in a city with an NHL franchise. All North American amateur players from the age of 18 to 20 years old and European amateurs from 18 to 21 years old are eligible.
- The University of Michigan hockey team has won the most NCAA titles (nine).
- Gretzky may have been the greatest player of all-time, but Gordie Howe was "Mr. Hockey." Howe first played in the NHL for the Detroit Red Wings in 1946 and ended his career with the Hartford Whalers in 1980. He later played a single game for a minor league team in 1997.
- The World Hockey Association (WHA) attempted to challenge the NHL when it was formed in 1971. Although it folded in 1979, many of its teams became NHL expansion franchises including the Winnipeg Jets, Edmonton Oilers, Hartford Whalers, and Quebec Nordiques.

TIME FOR A COCKTAIL

For many people, booze is a crucial appendage of any sport, but for some, it is a sport in itself. I'm not talking about drinking games necessarily, although those can be fun and certainly are sport to many, but more so the science and art behind making and consuming specific drinks. We'll get to the specifics behind distilled liquors, beer, and wine in other sections, but for now let's talk about Long Island Iced Teas, Harvey Wallbangers, and Prairie Fires.

That's right, let's talk about cocktails and mixed drinks.

A cocktail is simply a concoction that includes one or more distilled drinks/spirits, and/or some beer or wine, and some non-alcoholic mixer for flavor. With bar orientated television shows like *Bar Rescue* being quite popular right now, mixed drinks have become the rage in bars across the United States.

The evolution toward cocktails began in the 1600s and 1700s with julep, toddies, and other simple drinks. While these are still considered cocktails, they certainly aren't as complicated as they are today.

The oldest published reference to a cocktail goes back to 1803, but the name itself isn't explained. There are many possible explanations, ranging from the Aztec word for flower "Xochitl," to feathers from a rooster's tail being served with drinks as a garnish.

Random Facts:

- A hot toddy is simply a drink made from whisky, water, and honey and served hot, often garnished with a slice of fruit.
- The oldest known reference to a "cocktail" was in the *Farmer's Cabinet* from 1803. It states: "Drank a glass of cocktail—excellent for the head." It isn't known if the drink referred to was alcoholic.
- Angostura Bitters is traditionally one of the ingredients in early cocktails. Bitters is simply an alcoholic drink that has been flavored with herbs or other plants.
- Cocktail parties became popular in the United States from the 1950s to the mid-1960s. The host or hostess would serve a variety of cocktails and the guests would dress neatly: men wore coats and ties and women wore "cocktail dresses." Cocktail dresses are considered semi-formal dresses.
- Another potential origin for the word "cocktail" comes from James Fennimore Cooper's 1821 novel, *The Spy*. In the novel, which takes place during the American Revolution, one of the main characters serves some French soldiers drinks that are garnished with the tail feathers of a rooster.
- A Harvey Wallbanger consists of vodka, Galliano (or a similar liqueur), and orange juice. The drink was invented by Los Angeles mixologist Donato Antone in 1952 and named for a local surfer.
- A good cocktail server doesn't just have a library of drink ingredients in their head, they know the art of "flairing." "Flairing" refers to unique and catchy ways the bartender pours the drinks, which can include juggling, shaking the cocktail shaker seductively, or even doing magic tricks.
- The 1988 film *Cocktail* starred Tom Cruise as a bartender who learns the tricks of the trade, including flair, from a veteran of the

business. Although it was critically panned, *Cocktail* did well in the box office.

- If you're an American or Canadian visiting a bar or restaurant in Europe, remember not to tip your bartender! It's more of a choice whether you tip in Europe, but most people don't because bartenders are paid a standard wage. They'll like you if you do, though!
- Grog is a drink comprised of rum or whisky mixed with water. It was issued to British sailors in the 1700s and although the exact origins of the term are unknown, it may have to do with the British Admiral Edward Vernon (1684-1757), who was known as "Old Grog" because he wore a grogram coat.
- Ada Coleman (1875-1966) was a pioneer in the drinking world. She was one of only two women to be the head bartender at the Savoy Hotel in London, and she invented the "Hanky Panky" cocktail.
- After Prohibition ended, with new alcohol laws enacted in each state, bartender schools popped up across the United States. Students at bartending schools learn how to make mixed drinks and are awarded a certificate or license upon completion, although requirements to have a certificate or license to tend bar vary from jurisdiction to jurisdiction.
- A Long Island Iced Tea is made from equal parts vodka, tequila, gin, rum triple sec, 1 ½ parts sour mix, and a splash of cola.
- The Old Fashioned is a standard cocktail, and as the name indicates, one of the oldest on record. It's made by mixing sugar with bitters, whisky, and then pouring over ice and garnished with a slice of fruit.
- The fictional British spy hero James Bond likes his Martinis "shaken, not stirred," which is shown to be somewhat healthier since it has more antioxidants. With that said, many bartenders

think that a true Martini should never be shaken since clear cocktails should usually be stirred. Some bartenders also believe that shaking the mix bruises the gin, thereby hurting the flavor of the Martini.

- A "shooter" is a mixed drink "shot." Shooters that are true cocktails are usually sweet and colorful, such as the Lemon Drop, which is made from vodka, lemon juice, triple sec, and syrup.
- A Prairie Fire can be served as a standard cocktail or a shooter. It is normally made from whisky and hot sauce in a 1:1 or 1:2 mixture. Prairie Fires are popular in the American South and Midwest.
- The bar business can be costly to get into, averaging between $110,000 and $550,000, but the lure of big money keeps it going. Average bars bring in between $25,000 to $30,000 per week and the overall revenue for American bars in 2018 was $28 billion. It is estimated that distilled drinks and cocktails make up about 31% of that revenue.
- *The Fine Art of Mixing Drinks* by David A. Embry was one of the first true cocktail guides. Written in 1948, Embry detailed not only the ingredient of drinks but also their categories and the settings in which they should be served.
- If you're feeling a little tired the next time you go out to the bar or club with your friends, try having an Irish Coffee. A true Irish Coffee cocktail is made from Jameson or another Irish whisky, coffee, sugar, and topped with cream. Remember, though, not to swirl the cream as you are supposed to drink the cocktail through it.

THE GRAND SLAMS

When most Americans hear the term "grand slam" they probably think of baseball, or maybe breakfast at Denny's, but the rest of the world thinks of tennis. In the tennis world, "Grand Slam" refers to the four "major" tennis tournaments of a calendar year: the Australian Open, the French Open, Wimbledon, and the U.S. Open. These are the four most prestigious tournaments in professional tennis and have the highest prize purses.

If a player can win just one of these tournaments, it's a big deal, but winning all four, especially in a calendar year, is legendary. Although there is no official "Grand Slam" title, it is technically applied to those who win all four tournaments in a calendar year.

There are several ways to win the Grand Slam. There's a men's singles division, a women's singles division, a men's doubles division, a women's doubles division, and a mixed doubles division. No player has yet to win all four singles, doubles, and mixed doubles tournaments in a calendar year, although some have done so over a career.

Australian Margaret Court won 24 Grand Slam singles titles during her career and completed the single year/true Grand Slam three times in her career—once in singles and twice in mixed doubles—which is the most among all players. Her fellow Australian Rod Laver is second in total Grand Slams with two, both in singles competition.

Random Facts:

- Four players have won at least four Grand Slam events in a row—Novak Djokovic, Martina Navratilova, Steffi Graf, and Serena Williams—but only Graf won the true Grand Slam in a calendar year. Navratilova won six Grand Slam events in a row, the 1983 Wimbledon to the 1984 US Open, but was unable to win the big four in a calendar year.
- The Grand Slams begin with the Australian Open in January. Because Australia is in the Southern Hemisphere, January is the middle of the summer Down-Under. The French Open is in late May or early June, Wimbledon is in late June or early July, and the US Open is usually during Labor Day weekend.
- In addition to the standard men's, women's, and doubles' divisions, there are wheelchair divisions in the Grand Slam tournaments.
- Wimbledon, also known as "The Championships," is the oldest of the Grand Slam events, beginning in 1877.
- Swiss tennis player Martina Hingis was the last non-wheelchair athlete to win the calendar-year Grand Slam. She won the Grand Slam in women's doubles in 1998.
- The "Golden Grand Slam" is when a tennis player wins a gold medal in addition to the four Grand Slam events in a year. German Steffi Graf is the only tennis player so far to have achieved this feat (1988).
- The "Open Era" of tennis began in 1968. Before that only amateurs could compete in International Tennis Federation tournaments, which included all of the current Grand Slam Events. Because of that, some statisticians place an asterisk after Rod Laver's first Grand Slam (1962) but not his second (1969).

- Margaret Court's mixed doubles (1963, 1965) Grand Slams came before the Open Era, but her singles Grand Slam (1970) was earned in the Open Era.
- Besides the stiff competition and far removed settings, the differences in courts make winning a calendar Grand Slam, or even a cumulative Grand Slam, difficult. The US and Australian Opens are on hardcourt, the French Open is on clay, and Wimbledon is on grass.
- The Australian Open is the newest Grand Slam tournament, first starting in 1905. Since 1988, it has been played at Melbourne Park.
- Prize money is awarded similarly in each of the Grand Slam Events, with players earning more money the farther they advance in the tournaments. Although men and women only compete against each other in the mixed doubles division, the pay is equal throughout. The singles winner makes nearly $4 million at the US Open, $2.5 million at Wimbledon, $2.5 million at the French Open, and $2.8 million at the Australian Open.
- The French Open dates back to 1891, but it wasn't designated a major until 1924 when all four tournaments were considered together as the four biggest events in tennis.
- Due to Australia being so far away from North America and Europe, the Australian Open was often skipped by tennis players before the Open Era.
- American Don Budge (1915-2000) was the first person to win a calendar-year Grand Slam in 1938.
- American tennis player Venus Williams is known for her killer serves and athleticism and overall successful career. She has won seven singles Grand Slam tournaments, but she never won the calendar Grand Slam. Williams made it to the finals of the Australian twice but lost and the French Open once but lost. The clay surface of the French Open slows down the ball, which hurts power players such as Williams.

- The French Open is also known as "Roland Garros" because it's held in the Roland Garros stadium in Paris, France.
- The US Open is the second-oldest of the four tournaments, beginning play in 1881. It was played on grass until 1974, then on clay until 1978, and has been a hardcourt ever since.
- Swiss Roger Federer has won more Grand Slam tournaments (20) than any other male player and has won all four tournaments, but he hasn't won them all in the same year.
- Serena Williams is number two all-time in total Grand Slam tournament wins (23), male or female, one behind Margaret Court. Williams has won all four tournaments and did so in the Open Era, but like Federer, she hasn't won all four in the same calendar year.
- Since the late 1980s, tennis players and fans often refer to the Australian Open as the "Happy Slam." It's gained this nickname through the locals' friendly, laid-back attitude and the money the country has put into the tournament. It also helps that it's a nice break from the winter of the Northern Hemisphere.

HOW DID BASKETBALL GO GLOBAL?

We discussed earlier in this book how association football is the most popular sport in the world but is number five at best in the United States. Of those other four sports, which do you think is the biggest American export?

Well, outside of the United States, gridiron football is only popular north of the border, and based on its history, you could argue that it was the Canadians who exported it to the US in the first place. And hockey truly is a Canadian export.

So, that leaves baseball then, right? After all, baseball is the most popular sport in many Asian and Latin American countries and is number two or three in several more. Baseball has also been played in many countries outside the United States for decades.

But as much as baseball is America's game, it's not the US's number one sports export. No, that would be basketball.

Basketball may have gotten a late start in the international arena, but it's now the second-most popular sport in the world. Over one billion people follow basketball worldwide and the sport generates over $4.75 billion in revenue. It's second in the number of professional leagues behind association football and it is number one in average player salaries.

International players are on just about every National Basketball Association (NBA) roster and have been for years. If you're even a little familiar with basketball, then you know the names Dirk Nowitzki, Yao Ming, Manu Ginboli, and the Gasol brothers, Pau and Marc.

Truly, basketball is America's number one sports export.

Random Facts:

- Although basketball began in the United States, it had international influences from the beginning. Canadian-born Jim Naismith is credited as the inventor of basketball when he introduced it to the school where he taught in Springfield, Massachusetts as an indoor activity for the winter and rainy days.
- Basketball was introduced into the Philippines by American Marines, sailors, and soldiers in the early 1900s. It's now the most popular sport in the country and has been home to the professional Philippine Basketball Association since 1975.
- The International Basketball Federation (FIBA) was founded in 1932 as the organization that defines the rules of basketball internationally. It organizes all international basketball tournaments, including the Olympics.
- Sudan-born Manute Bol (1962-2010) was one of the first Africans to play in the NBA and at 7'6 was also one of the tallest.
- The Soviet Union's basketball team was one of the most successful Olympic teams in history. It competed in nine Olympics, winning two gold medals, four silver medals, and three bronze medals. The Soviet team competed in nine FIBA World Cup tournaments and 21 FIBA EuroBasket tournaments.
- The EuroLeague is a professional basketball league comprised of 18 teams across Europe. In terms of player talent, fan support, and revenue, EuroLeague is second of all basketball leagues only to the NBA.
- Although the game of basketball is essentially the same throughout the world, it is played a bit differently in Europe than in the United States. The game is quicker in America than Europe, which is partially due to some small differences in rules, including

a shorter three-point line in Europe, "traveling" is called far less in the NBA, and far fewer fouls are called in Europe.

- The tallest listed NBA player in history was also international. Romanian Gheorge Mureşan was listed at 7'7.
- One of the greatest—and chippiest—international basketball games of all time was the 1972 gold medal game between the Soviet Union and the United States. The Americans were a heavy favorite, but the Soviets brought their "A" game and also played rough, getting into the Americans' heads and causing two Americans to get ejected. The Soviets won the game 51-50 on a last-second shot.
- Pétur Karl Guðmundsson is a mountain of a man, standing 7'2. The Icelander was seemingly made for basketball. Although he only played one year for the Portland Trailblazers (1981-1982), he was the first Icelander and was also the first European to be given an NBA contract.
- Liga ACB is the top basketball league in Spain and the second-best in Europe. It functions somewhat like association football, with 18 teams playing a season and the two worst teams "relegated" at the end of the season to a lower league.
- When center Luc Longley was drafted by the Minnesota Timberwolves in 1991, he became the first Australian to play in the NBA.
- Besides the EuroLeague, there are three other European-wide basketball competitions. The Euro Cup is the second-tier of the EuroLeague, while the Champions League is the FIBA equivalent of the EuroLeague and the Europe Cup is FIBA's second tier competition. Teams qualify for these leagues based on their standings in national leagues, which means the teams in each league can change drastically from year to year.
- American Allen Iverson played 14 years in the NBA on his way to the Basketball Hall of Fame, but ended his career with Beşiktaş J.K. of the Turkish Super League.

- NCAA/college basketball is extremely popular in the United States, but in recent years, with the worldwide increase in the popularity of basketball, American college teams have done pre-season tours in foreign countries. An American college team is allowed to do one pre-season, foreign tour every four years and can only play a maximum of ten games per tour.
- Basketball is the most popular sport in China. Besides Yao Ming, five other Chinese nationals have played in the NBA.
- The average EuroLeague salary is about $60,000 with the top players earning around $100,000. In contrast, the minimum NBA salary is more than $800,000.
- Perhaps not surprisingly, Canada has had more players in the NBA (49) than any other country other than the United States. Canada currently has one NBA franchise (Toronto Raptors) and from 1995 to 2001 had two (Vancouver Grizzlies), before the Grizzlies move to their current home in Memphis.
- Hank Biasatti (1922-1996) was born in Italy and later moved to Canada and become a Canadian citizen. In 1946 he became the first Canadian to play in the Basketball Association of America (which became the NBA) when he made the cut for the now-defunct Toronto Huskies.
- Sergei Belov (1944-2013), the Soviet player who scored the winning lay-up in the 1972 gold medal game against the United States, was named the FIBA best player of all-time in 1991 and was the first international player to be inducted into the Naismith Basketball Hall of Fame in 1992.

PING-PONG REALLY IS BIG IN CHINA

Most of you reading this probably don't consider table tennis/ping-pong to be a real sport. Sure, it can be fun and a good exercise of your reflexes and maybe even physically challenging, but a sport?

Well, to the Chinese, who know it as *pingpang*, it is one of their top sports and a way for them to demonstrate their athletic abilities to the world. Basketball may be the most popular sport in China, but ping-pong is where they dominate!

Since ping-pong became an official sport at the 1988 Summer Olympics, the Chinese have dominated, winning 28 of 32 gold medals and 53 medals in 32 events. There is little doubt that the Chinese love and dominate the world ping-pong scene and if you ever watch a high-level match, you'll see that these people are truly athletes.

But ping-pong's origins are quite humble and quite far removed from China.

Like many of the sports we've examined in this book, ping-pong originated in England in the 1800s as a recreational pastime and then spread throughout the world in the 1900s. By the time of the Chinese Civil War (1927-1936; 1945-1949), ping-pong was being played by the communist forces in their free time and after they took over the country, they made it the official sport of China.

The rest was sports history!

Random Facts:

- Do you remember when Forest Gump played the Chinese in ping-pong in the 1994 film *Forest Gump*? Although Forest Gump was a fictional character, the scene was based on a historic event known as "Ping-pong Diplomacy," which was a series of ping-pong matches between the Chinese and Americans in the early 1970s.
- Asian dominance in ping-pong began during the 1952 Ping-Pong Championships in Mumbai, India. The Japanese dominated, winning four gold medals, but Chinese leader Mao Zedong declared that ping-pong would be China's national sport.
- Ma Long from China is currently the third-ranked ping-pong player in the world and is considered by many to be the best player of all-time. He has been ranked number one for 64 months in his career and was at one time ranked first for 34 consecutive months. Long is the reigning Olympic and World champion.
- The top professional ping-pong league in China is the China Table Tennis Super League.
- Most of the non-Chinese Olympic ping-pong medals are won by players born in China. More than 124 Chinese born players have medaled for other countries.
- The International Table Tennis Federation (ITTF) was established in 1926 in Lausanne, Switzerland to oversee all ping-pong leagues.
- The Asian Table Tennis Association (ATTU) is the governing body for the Asian countries that are members of the ITTF. It was formed in 1975 and is based in Beijing, China. Each member country has a nation-wide association to oversee national league play; China's is the Chinese Table Tennis Association (CTTA).
- Ping-pong is also popular in Taiwan, which has made things interesting in international play with mainland China. Since

Taiwan is not officially recognized by most countries, it's called "Chinese Taipei" in competition.

- The 2007 American film *Balls of Fury* took a humorous look at the Chinese love of ping-pong. Film legend Christopher Walken played the protagonist, a ping-pong loving Chinese crime lord named Feng.
- Chinese ping-pong legend Zhuang Zedong (1940-2013) and American player Glenn Cowan (1952-2004) were the leading forces behind Ping-pong diplomacy. The two men met at a table tennis tournament in Japan in 1971.
- Although the vast majority of the players in the China Table Tennis Super League are native Chinese, a handful of foreign players have been in the league.
- Because China has dominated ping-pong so much at the international level, the rules in the summer Olympics were changed in 2012 so that only two players, or teams, from a single country can enter a particular category.
- In the Summer Olympics in Tokyo, there will be five ping-pong events: men's singles, men's team, women's singles, women's team, and mixed doubles.
- An important part of ping-pong is the way a player grips the racket. The "penhold" grip is the most popular style in East Asia and a variant of it is known as the "Chinese penhold."
- Lin Yun-ju is currently the top ping-pong player from Taiwan and is ranked sixth in the world.
- Deng Yaping is one of the best overall players in ping-pong history and is considered by many to be the best woman to have played the sport. She won 6 world championships and four Olympic gold medals in her career that lasted from 1989 to 1997.
- As China has become more capitalistic in recent years, they have

combined their excellence in ping-pong with profit. Beginning in 2011, they have offered four-year courses to foreigners to study the secrets of Chinese ping-pong.

- The top Chinese ping-pong players may be naturals, but they also train hard. Players usually train from November to April, six days a week for seven hours a day. In addition to training on the table with coaches, they also do physical exercises away from the table.
- When American President Richard Nixon visited China in February 1972, one of the stops he made was to a ping-pong exhibition in Beijing.
- Although the focus of Ping-pong Diplomacy was the matches between the US and China, the Chinese were willing to play just about any country. Mao's immediate goal was to enhance China's reputation in the world, but his long-term goals were to replace Taiwan as the internationally-recognized "China" and to slight the Soviet Union, as no Soviet ping-pong players were invited to China.

WILL THEY REALLY RAISE YOUR SPIRITS?

Earlier, we talked about mixed drinks and cocktails and how making them and consuming them is as much of a pastime as sports are for many people. The background of the hard liquor components of mixed drinks is a major story in itself, particularly the process used to make them and the history of that process.

So, why is hard liquor referred to as spirits?

Some believe that the answer to that question has to do with the distillation process. You see, liquor is unique from beer and wine because it is produced through the distillation process, which makes it stronger per ounce than other forms of alcohol. Without getting too technical, the distillation process is used to separate different chemicals through boiling and condensation, leaving the various drinks we know as alcohol.

In the middle ages, when distillation first began, it was believed that the vapor produced during the process was a "spirit" of the original substance.

Others believe that hard liquor began being called spirits because they were known to "lift the spirits" of those consuming the drinks.

Whatever the origins of the term, the distillation of liquor became a science in the early modern era. By the 1700s, various liquors were more popular in certain regions and countries than others: whisky in North America and the British Isles, vodka in Eastern Europe, and brandy in Western Europe.

Random Facts:

- Schnapps is the traditional liquor of the German-speaking world. After the alcohol is distilled, spices and syrups are added to give it its taste.
- The term "alcohol by volume" (ABV) is used to gauge the strength of a liquor. In addition to being distilled, many consider a proper spirit to be at least 20% ABV and to have no added sugar.
- Since many schnapps brands add sugar, they are often considered "liqueurs" instead of spirits.
- There are six major types of whiskies: Scotch, Irish, Bourbon, Tennessee, Canadian, Rye, and Japanese.
- The distillation process was discovered and used for different substances as far back as 1,200 BCE, but it was in the Middle Ages when the process was first used to make spirits. The Arab chemist and scholar Al-Kindi distilled wine in the 800s in modern-day Iraq.
- The process of "fractional distillation" is when a mixture is separated into its components.
- Is it "whiskey" or "whisky"? Well, "whiskey" used to be the preferred American spelling, but now many American companies, such as Maker's Mark, actually spell it as "whisky." American whisky is made with a mixture of grains not used in Europe and it's distilled three times before being stored.
- Brandy is a spirit that is made by distilling wine.
- A "mash" refers to a primary ingredient used to make the liquid in the distillation process of whisky. It's usually some type of grain that has been germinated in a process known as "malting." Bourbon always uses a corn mash.

- The ABV standard of determining an alcoholic drink's strength replaced the "proof" standard in many places. Both measures are still used in the United States, though, with proof being defined as twice the percentage of alcohol by volume. For example, if a vodka is 45% ABV, then it's 90 proof.

- Similar to whisky, vodka was originally distilled from the liquids of different grains. After potatoes were introduced to Europe from the Americas in the late 1600s, they began being used to create vodka.

- Alcohol is ethanol, which can also be used as a fuel source for our cars. The United States is the number one ethanol fuel producer in the world, with nearly all of that being produced in Iowa, Nebraska, Illinois, Minnesota, Indiana, and South Dakota.

- Baijiu is the main spirit of China. It's a clear drink that can be distilled from sorghum, rice, wheat, or barley.

- Gin is a spirit that uses juniper berries as its primary ingredient. It was first invented/discovered in England in the early 1600s and later become the popular spirit of southern England.

- Both bourbon and Tennessee whisky made from a corn mash and have a similar look and taste, but Tennessee whisky is filtered through charcoal before being placed in wooden casks for fermentation. A true whisky drinker will also tell you that bourbon has a sweeter taste. Whiskey snobs, and native Kentuckians, will also argue that true bourbon is only made in Kentucky.

- In Spain and Latin America, *aguardiente,* and in Portugal and Brazil, *aguardiente*, refers to a variety of strong alcoholic beverages that are fermented and distilled. They are usually made from fruits, but can also be derived from grains.

- Haiti has the highest per capita rate of spirit consumption at more than 99% of all alcohol consumed in that country.

- Bourbon was first produced in Bourbon County, Kentucky. The county was named in honor of King Louis XVI France for his role in aiding the Americans during the American Revolution. Although Kentucky has many "dry counties," Bourbon County isn't one of them.
- Rum is a spirit made from sugarcane molasses and sugarcane juice. Rum became popular in the Caribbean in the 1700s and is also the most popular spirit in the Canadian Atlantic provinces.
- Oghi is the most popular spirit in Armenia. It's distilled from fruits or berries and although sometimes thought of as "Armenian vodka," it's made with different ingredients and through a different process.
- Scotch is known for its "piney" or "earthy" flavor and is always made in Scotland.

CHAPTER 4:

Interesting History

Short but Important

When you look at most world leaders today, six feet is pretty much the standard height. Russian President Vladimir Putin often looks especially diminutive in the presence of other leaders, but he isn't particularly short at 5'7.

Throughout history, though, some pretty powerful people were also surprisingly short. But keep in mind, the average height of humans has increased steadily since ancient times.

Napoleon Bonaparte, the military genius and emperor of France in the late 1700s and early 1800s is often depicted as especially short. However, he was 5'6, which was pretty average for the time and isn't too far below average today. On the other hand, Winston Churchill is often viewed as larger than life, yet he too was 5'6. Perhaps his girth contributes to the perception that he was much taller.

Italian fascist dictator Benito Mussolini was also 5'6, while his buddy Hitler was listed as the above average for the time at 5'9.

There were a few leaders who truly were short by the standards of any time period.

Mexican President Benito Juarez (1806-1872) is listed at a tiny 4'6 and Israeli Prime Minister David Ben-Gurion (1886-1973) was only 5'0.

And as influential and beautiful as Cleopatra was, she is believed to have been a petite 5'0.

Random Facts:

- Benito Juarez was of Zapotec Indian descent, which would explain his height, as the Zapotecs tend to be smaller people.
- James Madison, who was the fourth American President from 1809-1817, was the shortest man to hold the office at 5'4.
- The height of Joseph Stalin, who was the leader of the Soviet Union from 1922 until he died in 1953, is disputed. Some sources list him at 5'4, while others have him as tall as 5'8.
- Although he was never the head of his country's government, Mahatma Gandhi (1869-1948) led India to independence. Gandhi was listed at 5'5.
- The late PLO leader Yasser Arafat (1929-2004) was only 5'2.
- Many people think that Mao Zedong, the first leader of Communist China was short, but he was 5'11.
- Kim Jong-un, the current leader of North Korea is 5'9, but his father and predecessor, Kim Jong-Il, only stood 5'3.
- Former Russian Prime Minister and President, Dimitri Medvedev, is only 5'4, which makes sense because Putin probably wouldn't want his right-hand man to be taller than him.
- Hideki Tojo, the Prime Minister of Japan for most of World War II, was 5'4. He was shorter than the world average at the time, but the average height for a Japanese soldier in World War II was only 5'3.
- Though not short for a woman, current German Chancellor Angela Merkel is usually among the shortest of world leaders in the room at 5'5.
- Alexander the Great is viewed today by many historians as the greatest conqueror in world history, but his deeds far outweighed

his height. Although not especially short, the towering personality stood 5′6.

- The height of the great Mongol ruler Genghis Khan (c. 1155-1227) has been the source of scholarly debate. There are no contemporary accounts that reference his height so people are left guessing for the most part.
- Spanish nationalist leader and later dictator of Spain, Francisco Franco (1892-1975), was called "El Paquito" or "Little Franc" because he stood just 5′3 or 5′4, depending on the source.
- On the opposite end of the spectrum, Maharana Patrap (1540-1597), the king of Mewar, is thought to have been the tallest leader in world history at 7′5. Despite being more than two feet taller than some of the people on our list, the shorter peoples' names are better remembered.
- The current President of Ireland, Michael D. Higgins, is listed as 5′3.
- Michell Bachaelet became the first female President of Chile in 2006 and was also her country's shortest leader, and the shortest in the world at the time, at 5′1.
- Iran's lightning rod former President Mahmoud Ahmadinejad's mouth and rhetoric often belied the fact that he only stands 5′2.
- Stalin's successor, Nikita Khrushchev (1894-1971), definitely was the shorter of the two dictators at 5′3.
- French leaders are generally not very tall on average at only 5′7, but former French President Nicholas Sarkozy is a little under that at 5′5.
- Queen Victoria of Britain (1819-1901) was only 5′0, but like her countryman Churchill, she made up for her lack of height with extra girth.

VIKINGS IN AMERICA?

With the recent Viking craze in television and movies, you probably know a few things about the Scandinavian warriors and explorers. You probably know that the Vikings, or Northmen as they were often called, founded colonies from England to Russia and engaged in long-distance trade with the Greeks, Arabs, and Persians.

But did you know the Vikings came to the Americas about 500 years before Christopher Columbus?

Norse sagas tell of a Viking colony in a place called "Vinland," which for centuries was believed to have been somewhere in late 10th and early 11th century North America, but it was never known for sure. Many doubted the existence of Vinland ("Grape Vine Land") until archaeologists discovered the remains of a Viking colony in L'Anse Aux Meadows, Newfoundland, Canada in the 1960s.

But just how extensive was Viking exploration and colonization in the Americas?

The fact that grapevines can't grow in L'Anse Aux Meadows and much of the flora and fauna described in the Viking sagas about North America is not native to Newfoundland has led many scholars to believe that a Viking colony—or colonies—existed far to the south in what is today the continental United States.

Unsubstantiated discoveries of Viking artifacts have been found as far west as Minnesota and Oklahoma, proving to some that the Vikings were quite prolific in their travels, while to others it simply shows that there are some pretty good hoaxers.

Random Facts:

- A coin of King Olaf of Norway (ruled 1066-1080) was found in Maine, proving to some that the Vikings traveled there. Skeptics argue that the coin could have ended up there in the modern period.
- A "runestone" is a stone inscribed in the runic script that Vikings often left in places they explored. More than one runestone has been discovered in North America.
- The most famous runestone discovered in America is known as the "Kensington Runestone." It was discovered by a farmer in 1898 in rural Douglas County, Minnesota and was supposedly left there by Scandinavian explorers in 1362.
- The Viking discovery of North America took place in stages. First, they colonized Iceland in the 9th century, then Greenland in the early 10th century, before moving onto what is now Canada in the late 10th century.
- Bjarni Hejolfsson was the first Viking to sight North America when he was blown off course from Greenland in 986.
- In 1923, the "Heavener Runestone" was first documented to have been discovered sometime earlier in Le Flore County, Oklahoma. There are six supposed runestones to have been found in Oklahoma altogether. As with the Kensington Runestone, most scholars believe they are fakes or that they were of a later settlement period.
- It is believed that Leif Eriksson was the first Scandinavian to have touched land in North America sometime around 1000 after being blown off course. Bjarni Herjólfsson was the first European to see America beyond Greenland, and the two unnamed shipwrecked men were the first people known to Europeans to have made landfall there.

- The Vikings knew Labrador and/or the Baffin Islands as "Helluland" (Rock Land), Newfoundland as Markland (Tree/Forest Land), and Vineland (Wine Land) was more than likely to the south.
- The northernmost limit of grape production in North America is the Gulf of St. Lawrence, which would fit the flora and fauna of the *Vinland Sagas.*
- The Narragansett Runestone is a large stone discovered in Rhode Island in the 1980s that is inscribed with two rows of mysterious symbols. Some believe the writing is runic, although Viking Age scholars are skeptical.
- The Vikings referred to American Indians as *Skraelings.*
- After Leif Eriksson set foot on land, the colony of L'Anse Aux Meadows was created.
- After Leif Eriksson's initial claim of Newfoundland, Thorfinn Karsefni was one of the most important Norse settlers and explorers of North America.
- The "Spirit Pond Runestones" are three small stones with supposed runic inscriptions found near Bath, Maine in 1971. Like the other discoveries in Minnesota, Oklahoma, and Rhode Island, scholars are skeptical but the locals believe they are proof the Vikings visited their area.
- Among all the runestones discovered in America, the Kensington Runestone is the most likely to be authentic, which is supported by several legitimate scholars.
- There would have been a somewhat clear course for Scandinavian explorers to reach Douglas County, Minnesota. They could have come down from the Hudson Bay to the Nelson River and then the Red River of the North to Minnesota. The course Norse explorers would have taken to get to Oklahoma isn't so clear, though.

- The Viking homes at L'Anse Aux Meadows were turf longhouses. At its peak, the population of the settlement was about 90 people with a boat repair shed and a blacksmith's shop.
- The "Elbow Lake Runestone" was a 1949 hoax runestone "discovered" near Barrett, Minnesota.
- In 1985, a group of students created an elaborate hoax when they claimed to have found a runestone where the Kensington Runestone was said to have been discovered. The students finally came forward in 2001 when talk of what became known as the AVM Runestone's authenticity began to be discussed.
- The L'Anse Aux Meadows colony was too far from Greenland, so around 1020, after only about 20 years of settlement, it was permanently abandoned.

ELEPHANT WARFARE

When Alexander the Great led his Macedonian-Greek army across the Indus River and into India in 326 BCE, it wouldn't be an understatement to say they entered a new world. The sights and sounds of India were unlike anything they knew in Europe or the Near East, and the Indians fought a style of warfare with which they were unfamiliar.

The Indians placed far less emphasis on cavalry and more on elephants.

Yes, elephants—those seemingly gentle giants—were used in warfare in India, and other places around the world, for centuries before and after the Greeks encountered them.

The ancient Aryan god of war, Indra, rode an elephant and as the myth goes, it was he who brought the idea of elephant warfare to India. From India, the concept of elephant warfare appears to have spread throughout Asia. Then some of Alexander's men brought the idea with them back to the West.

Pyrrhus, the king of the Greek-speaking kingdom of Epirus (ruled 297-272 BCE), used elephants to invade Italy in 280 BCE, and then Hannibal the ruler of Carthage did the same in 218 BCE.

The Romans successfully fought off the invaders and their elephants and then turned around and used war elephants against their enemies for nearly 200 years.

After the Roman Empire was established in 27 BCE, war elephants were a thing of the past in the West, but they continued to be used in Persia and India with varying degrees of success for the next 1,000 years.

Random Facts:

- War elephants had to be captured in the wild and couldn't be raised. They could only be tamed and never truly domesticated, which could cause problems on the battlefield if the elephants were spooked by trumpets and other sounds.
- The Asian elephant is the species that has been used primarily in warfare and exclusively in Persia, India, and East Asia.
- The Carthaginians and some of the Macedonian kingdoms used the now-extinct North African elephant. The North African elephant was smaller than the Asian elephant.
- An elephant team would consist of two to three men. The *mahout* was the driver of the elephant and along with him were one or two men who threw spears and/or shot arrows.
- The exact numbers of Pyrrhus' invasion force in Italy are not precise, but it was somewhere around 20,000 infantry, 3,000 cavalry, and dozens of elephants.
- When the Vietnamese used elephant troops in the Sino-French War (1884-1885), it was the last major engagement of elephant warfare.
- In 217 BCE, the Battle of Raphia was fought on June 22 between Ptolemaic Egypt led by Ptolemy IV and the Seleucid Empire led by Antiochus III. The Seleucids had more than 100 war elephants and the Ptolemies over 70, but the Ptolemies won the battle.
- When a mass of war elephants was used in a battle, they were usually placed at the center. Since they weren't as maneuverable as horses, they really couldn't be used for flanking operations.
- The Battle of Zama took place in 202 BCE between the Hannibal led Carthaginians and the Romans led by Scipio. The Carthaginians had the advantage with more than 80 war elephants, but when they

charged, Scipio simply ordered the center of the Roman forces to move and let them keep running. It worked!

- Hannibal rode an elephant named "Surus," which is believed to be a Punic (Carthaginian) word for "Syrian," perhaps indicating that it was a Syrian elephant. The Syrian elephant was a subspecies of the Asian elephant that is now extinct.
- Opposing forces used a variety of tactics to hurt and scare elephants. Drums and trumpets were often used and when those didn't work, armies would sometimes try to attack their legs.
- Elephants would be fitted with some armor, but not too much since the wild beasts didn't react well to such restrictions. Special swords, called "tusk swords," were often placed on the ends of their tusks.
- Elephants played a critical role in the military of the Mauryan Empire (323-184 BCE), comprising one of the six divisions of the army.
- At its peak, the Mauryan Empire had the largest recorded elephant force with more than 9,000 elephants.
- Elephants once ranged from Mesopotamia (Iraq) in the west to China in the east. A combination of hunting and deforestation led to their extinction in those regions.
- Only male elephants could be used in warfare. Females are not necessarily less tough or aggressive than males, but they will always run from male elephants, which made them useless in elephant-on-elephant warfare.
- The Mong Mao state used about 100 elephants against the Chinese Ming Dynasty during the Ming-Mong Mao War (1386-1388). The Ming Dynasty won the war and the Ming- Mong Mao state lost about half its elephants. It was the last major war in China in which war elephants were used.

- Although the movie *300* depicts the Achaemenid Persians using war elephants against the Greeks at the Battle of Thermopylae in 480 BCE, the first time on record the Persians used elephants against the Greeks was at the Battle of Gaugamela in 331 BCE.
- The Romans used war elephants against each other during the Civil Wars of the 1st century BC. The Battle of Thapsus in 46 BCE was the last major battle in which Romans used elephants.
- After the Persian Sassanid Empire was defeated in 651 CE by the Arab Muslims, elephant warfare was only used sporadically throughout the world.

BEHIND ENEMY LINES

An unfortunate aspect of world history is that it's littered with unknown human bodies that have been unclaimed in numerous wars. War is a regrettable yet important part of human history, so knowing why and how those wars were fought is an important part of understanding humanity.

Most major wars involved large armies taking part in large-scale maneuvers and battles that left thousands dead at a time. These types of major battles could decide the course of a war overnight and end a war rather quickly.

Then there are the wars where one side is seriously underfunded, undermanned, and overwhelmed. If groups in this position want to put up any serious resistance, they are forced to resort to "asymmetrical" or "irregular" tactics. Often called "guerilla warfare," these tactics include ambush and hit and run attacks, sabotage, and blending into the surrounding environment, rural or urban.

Guerilla warfare has been used since the dawn of human civilization, but its peak was during the Cold War when the major superpowers funded and used guerilla groups as proxies against their larger enemies.

Guerilla groups can still be found around the world and will continue to exist whenever a smaller force comes into conflict with a large nation and army that they cannot hope to win against in a conventional war. The general strategy of any guerilla force is to make the occupation of their land non-worthwhile by inflicting small but repeated casualties on the enemy. Because of this strategy, guerilla warfare is sometimes referred to as "death by 1,000 papercuts" and "the war of flea."

Random Facts:

- The term "guerilla warfare" is derived from the French word for "war"—*guerre.*
- In pre-modern times, guerillas could sabotage occupying armies by poisoning wells and burning fields, thereby depriving them of food and water.
- The first leader of Communist China, Mao Zedong (1893-1976), detailed a modern history of guerilla warfare events and tactics in his 1937 book *On Guerilla Warfare.*
- Mao's book and theories were heavily influenced by those of Chinese writer Sun Tzu, who although wrote his *The Art of War* in the 6th century BCE, advocated some elements of guerilla warfare.
- The term "partisan" is often used interchangeably for 'guerilla', especially in Eastern Europe.
- Since guerillas usually don't wear uniforms and aren't part of official armies, they are often not given the same privileges as soldiers from official armies when captured.
- The line between "terrorism" and guerilla warfare is often blurred since the definition of terrorism varies widely and guerillas have used tactics often associated with terrorists, including bombings.
- When Napoleon and the French army invaded Russia in 1812, they were beaten by a combination of the elements and guerilla warfare. As they made their long trek out of Russia through the snow, they were ambushed by Russian partisans.
- The Boers used guerilla tactics against the British in the Second Boer War (1899-1902) in South Africa that included cutting telegraph lines and sabotaging railroads.
- Notable Argentine communist revolutionary Ernesto "Che"

Guevara (1928-1967) wrote a 1961 book about guerilla warfare titled *Guerilla Warfare*. The book drew heavily on Guevara's success in the Cuban Revolution (1953-1959).

- Although most modern guerilla groups have been left-wing in ideology, some have been anti-communist. The Forest Brothers were Baltic anti-communist guerillas who waged asymmetrical warfare against the Soviet Union from 1944 to 1956.
- In the final days of World War II, some of the Nazis planned to continue to resist the allies in a guerilla campaign known as "Operation Werewolf." Werewolf attacks were limited, but reprisals by the Red Army in the east were severe.
- After the Carthaginian General Hannibal defeated Rome in nearly every conventional battle and devastated southern Italy, Roman General Quintus Fabius Maximus Verrucosus devised the "Fabian Strategy," which was to only engage Hannibal in small-scale battles and ambushes.
- The "Contras" (Spanish -"against") were one of the more notable anti-communist guerilla groups during the Cold War. The Contras were supported by the United States and fought against the communist government of Nicaragua in the 1980s.
- The Vietcong was one of the most notable and successful guerilla groups of the 20th century. Their ambushes, traps, and tunnels were one of the many reasons why the Americans eventually left Vietnam in 1975.
- After traveling with Che Guevara and Fidel Castro during the Cuban Revolution, American journalist Robert Taber (1919-1995), wrote *The War of the Flea: The Classic Study of Guerilla Warfare*. The book chronicles the history of the revolution as well as the successful guerilla tactics used.
- The Irish Republican Army has been accused of being a terrorist group, but claims to be guerillas and "freedom fighters." Their

attacks on British military and police outposts certainly fit the guerilla definition, but their bombings of civilian targets meet most definitions of terrorism.

- Bleeding Kansas (1854-1861) was essentially a civil war in Kansas Territory between pro-slavery guerillas known as "Border Ruffians" and anti-slavery/free-soil guerillas called "Jayhawkers."
- The American Civil War (1861-1865) was primarily a conventional war between the Union and Confederate armies, but there was a considerable amount of guerilla warfare in the border states. Quantrill's Raiders was the name of one of the most notorious pro-Confederate guerilla groups, which included famous American outlaws Jesse and Frank James among their numbers.
- The North Atlantic Treaty Organization (NATO) and the CIA developed a program known as "stay-behind" operations during the Cold War where they trained, funded, and supplied right-wing organizations with weapons. The theory was that NATO would be driven from Europe by the Soviet Union, but that right-wing groups would stay behind and engage in guerilla activity.

MEDITATE ON IT

One of the most important aspects of any culture in world history, especially in the pre-modern world, is religion. Religion is how a culture defines its world and attempts to explain the unexplainable. It helps people understand some of the mysteries of life and what may happen after life.

As religion became more important, different sects formed and within many of those sects, the most pious men and women decided that the best way to serve god was to do so away from the influences of the world. The places where these pious individuals gathered became known as monasteries, the men who lived in them became known as "monks," the women were "nuns," and their way of life became known as "monasticism."

Monasticism revolves around monks and nuns doing communal chores at the monastery and praying. They abstain from sex, mood-altering chemicals, and most worldly possessions. Monasticism has played an important role in Christian history, beginning in Egypt in the 4th century and becoming a part of the Roman Catholic Church in the 6th century. Today, monastic orders can be found in the Catholic, Anglican, and all Orthodox churches.

Buddhism, Hinduism, and Jainism have even longer traditions of monasticism, dating back to the 5th century BCE.

Although monastic orders try to separate themselves from greater society as much as possible, they've played an important role in history. Monasteries have traditionally served as libraries and therefore have been the source of much centuries-old knowledge. The early Western European monasteries preserved ancient Roman texts and are one of the major reasons why Europe survived the Dark Ages.

Monasteries of any religion were places where followers focused on improving their minds, bodies, and spirits.

Random Facts:

- The Coptic/Egyptian Orthodox Church is steeped in the monastic tradition. The first Christian monk is believed to have been Anthony the Great (251-356 CE), who went to the desert to live as an "ascetic," or one who practices self-denial.
- Buddhism was essentially a religion founded on monastic and ascetic principles. The founder of the religion, Gautama Buddha, practiced self-denial and although he chose to live within the greater society, he helped establish Buddhist monastic orders.
- Roman Catholic monasticism can be traced to the Italian monk, Benedict of Nursia (480-550 CE), who founded monasteries and wrote *The Rule of St. Benedict* in 516 CE. *The Rule* became the essential guide for monks and nuns in the Catholic Church.
- In most Christian traditions, the male head of a monastery is known as an "Abbot," while a female head is an "Abbess."
- Zen Buddhism monks and nuns are allowed to marry when they reach a higher level of ordination. This practice has spread to other areas of East Asia but remains rare in Buddhism.
- The Hindu equivalent of a monk is a "*Sadu*" and a Hindu nun is a "*Sadhvi*."
- There are no monastic orders or monasteries in Islam, as it's a religion that promotes its followers to live in and influence greater society. The closest thing to an Islamic monk would be Sufis, who do practice asceticism, but they generally take part in the world.
- In the Roman Catholic Church, "mendicant orders" were comprised of monks who practiced self-denial but lived in society. The Franciscans started as a mendicant order.
- In the Coptic Church, the "Desert Fathers and Mothers" refers to the first monks and nuns who retreated to the deserts in the 3rd century to build some of the first monasteries.

- A Buddhist monk is known as a *"Bhikkhu,"* while a nun is a *Bhikkhuni."*
- In Christian monastic tradition, a "cenobite" is an ascetic who lives and works with others like himself in a monastery, while an "eremitic" is a hermit.
- The most impressive of all Coptic monasteries is the Monastery of St. Anthony. It was built over the grave of Anthony the Great in 251 CE about 208 miles southeast of Cairo in the Eastern Desert.
- Monks of the Digambara sect of Jainism take the idea of self-denial very seriously. They consider any clothing a possession so they are nude at all times and use a peacock feather to brush aside any insects on their pathway.
- Monasticism historically has not played a very important role in Judaism, although the Nazirites were a group in the Old Testament who voluntarily separated from greater society.
- One of the best-known Buddhist examples of monasticism in the West are the Shaolin monks. The Shaolin monks are Chan/Zen monks. The primary Shaolin monastery, known as the Shaolin Temple, is located in the Henan Province of China.
- The Byzantine Empire had a long tradition of monasticism in the Middle Ages and served as a bridge between the Orthodox and Roman Catholic worlds.
- The Essenes were a Jewish sect that existed from the 2nd century BCE to the 1st century CE. They lived communally and apart from greater society and generally practiced self-denial.
- Communist governments in Eastern Europe and China often targeted monastic orders with repression, but they continued to exist and do so in those countries to this day. The Shaolin monks in particular were beaten and humiliated during China's Cultural Revolution (1966-1976).

- Buddhist "stupas" were the locations where the relics of important monks and nuns were kept and also where monks and nuns would mediate.
- Roman Catholicism has several different monastic orders, with the Benedictines being the oldest. They were founded by St. Benedict in 529 CE in Monte Cassino, Italy.

A HORSE IS A HORSE, OF COURSE, OF COURSE

Although the horse became practically obsolete in most industrialized countries more than 70 years ago, it remains one of the most cherished of all humanity's animal companions. Horses are still kept as pets, they are raced in competitions, and they are also the subject of pop culture: in case you didn't know, the title of this section is from the theme song of the 1960s sitcom, *Mr. Ed,* which was about a talking horse.

So, why this love of horses?

Well, horses have helped different groups of humans in war and work, helping build civilization from the ground up. Archaeology shows that the first horses were domesticated just after 4,800 BCE on the Pontic-Caspian steppes (the area of modern Ukraine and Russia north of the Caucus Mountains) by Indo-European nomads.

You may be surprised that the first horses were used for meat!

Living on the steppes is tough, so the early Indo-Europeans needed a reliable source of meat. Sheep will forage through soft snow for grass, but not ice, and cattle won't even attempt to do that if they can't see snow. But horses are smarter and will use their hooves to break through ice to get to the snow.

After horses were tamed, they could then be tied to wagons. The wheel was needed for this next development. Then, so horses could be used more effectively in warfare, the first spoked wheel chariots were invented.

The earliest known chariots are also traced to the steppes just after 4,000 BCE. From there, the concept of the chariot moved south into the Near East where the Egyptians, Hittites, and other Bronze Age peoples made them famous.

Random Facts:

- Horses may have been ridden by single riders at an early point in their domestication, but true cavalry wasn't practiced until the Assyrians did so in the 9th century BCE.
- The primary reason why chariots came before cavalry was due to the relatively slight size of horses in the Bronze Age.
- An Egyptian chariot had two wheels with six spokes and a leather cab; they were usually pulled by two horses but could be pulled by four or more. The chariot team consisted of a shield-bearer, who also controlled the reigns, and an archer.
- A Hittite chariot resembled Egyptian chariots in most ways, except they had three-man teams: a driver, a shield-bearer, and a spearman.
- The Przewalski's horse is a wild horse species native to the steppes that is genetically similar to the first domesticated horses. It is the only true wild horse species left on Earth.
- The "war wagon" was the predecessor of the chariot, which was used by the Sumerians in Mesopotamia in the 4th millennium BCE. A war wagon had four solid wheels and was pulled by three or more horses.
- The wheel was probably invented independently in multiple places in the Near East and the steppes, but it was more than likely being by the late Neolithic Period, around 6,500 BCE.
- The earliest known chariots have been excavated from graves of the Sintashta culture (c. 2,200-1,800 BCE) in southern Russia. The Sintashta were Indo-Europeans who mined copper and bronze in addition to making the first chariots.
- The use of the chariot spread quickly throughout the Near East after 1,500 BCE. It is believed by many that the Mitanni Kingdom

(c, 1,500-1,350 BCE), which was located in what is now northern Iraq and Syria, played a major role in that diffusion.

- The chariot was brought into India around 1,500 BCE by the Aryans.
- Chariots may look more imposing than cavalry, but they were much more expensive to maintain because more horses were needed and skilled workers were needed to repair or build new chariots. A single rider on a horse is also much more maneuverable than a chariot team.
- The Assyrian King Tukulti-ninurta II (ruled 890-884 BCE) was the first to record using cavalry as "horsemen who go at my side."
- A relief from the Egyptian King Horemheb's rule (c. 1,323-1,295 BCE) shows one of the earliest known examples of a single rider on a horse. The bareback rider is probably not too uncommon for the Late Bronze Age, although such riders would have been used as scouts and not cavalry.
- The 17,000-year-old cave paintings in Lascaux, France are famous for the many realistic depictions of late Paleolithic animals. Several small horses are shown, although they were species that probably went extinct and weren't directly related to those that were later domesticated.
- Wild mares were easier to domesticate than wild stallions.
- In addition to being the first people to develop cavalry, the Assyrians were probably also the first people to invent the saddle. The early Assyrian saddle was quite primitive, though, consisting of little more than a cloth held in by some straps.
- The Botai culture was a steppe culture that existed from 3,700 to 3,100 BCE in what is today Kazakhstan. They practiced early horse domestication and may have ridden horses to hunt horses.
- The consumption of horse meat faded as they became more useful

for war and transportation, but it didn't go away. Nearly five million horses are slaughtered worldwide for food, with nearly two million in China alone.

- The most important factors that lead to the domestication of the horse were that it met six crucial prerequisites: efficient diet, quick growth rate, ability to breed in captivity, pleasant disposition, calm under pressure, and a social structure.
- The chariot continued to be used in warfare, with some modifications, after the invention of cavalry. The Persians invented the "scythed chariot," which was simply scythed blades on the wheels of the chariots. Once Alexander the Great defeated the Persians, though, chariots were relegated to ceremonial and recreational use.

THESE WOMEN WORE THE PANTS IN THEIR HOUSES

Although it may be true that most leaders throughout world history have been men, there have also been a considerable number of women, from nearly every culture and period, who have also played major roles in shaping our world. Female queens, prime ministers, and even military leaders have stood alongside the men of their time, earning their respect by effectively leading their people.

No doubt you've heard of Cleopatra, the last queen of Egypt, Joan of Arc of France, and British Prime Minister Margaret Thatcher. But have you heard of Hatshepsut (c. 1,507-1,458 BCE), an Egyptian queen who rose to power to rule Egypt as a *pharaoh* later in her life?

Or what about Wu Zetian (624-705 CE)? Wu ruled as the power behind the throne in Zhou China before pulling a "Hatshepsut" and openly ruling as the empresses of China.

The Middle Ages and early modern period brought us Queen Isabella I of Castile (1454-1504), who is credited with being the force behind unifying Christian Spain, expelling the Muslims from the Iberian Peninsula, and taking a gamble on a guy named Christopher Columbus. The gamble that she took on Columbus led to Spain becoming the world's preeminent power for more than 200 years.

So, let's take a look at a few more of these amazing women and some of their important feats.

Random Facts:

- German-born Catherine the Great was the Empress of Russia from 1762 to 1796. She is credited with modernizing Russia and making it one of the great European powers.
- Cleopatra (ruled 51-30 BCE) was an ethnic Macedonian Greek. She was a member of the Ptolemy family that began ruling Egypt in 305 BCE after Alexander the Great conquered the Near East.
- Benazir Bhutto (1953-2007) was notable for being the first woman to lead a Muslim country when she became Pakistan's prime minister from 1988 to 1990 and again from 1993 to 1996. She was assassinated in 2007.
- Although European kings and queens were for the most part figureheads by the 1880s, Queen Victoria (1819-1901) of the United Kingdom was so important she had a period in British history named after her (Victorian England/Britain). The Victorian Era was marked by high moral standards and the beginning of social reforms.
- Isabella married Ferdinand II, the King of Aragon, in 1469 to unite the two most powerful kingdoms in northern Spain.
- Margaret Thatcher entered British politics in the late 1950s and by 1975 she was leading the Conservative Party as the opposition. When the Conservatives became the majority party in parliament in 1979, she was elected prime minister.
- Catherine the Great had to learn a new language and religion before she could become ruler of Russia. She was baptized and raised Lutheran and knew no Russian until she moved to Russia and married Peter III in 1745.
- A woman named Zenobia was the queen of the merchant empire of Palmyra from 267-272 BCE.

- Indira Gandhi (1917-1984) was the third prime minister of India and the country's first and only female prime minister. She was assassinated by her Sikh bodyguards.
- Theodora (500-548 CE) was the wife of the Byzantine Empire's greatest ruler, Justinian I (ruled 527-565 CE). She is said to have influenced his decisions on many of Byzantium's successful domestic policies, which included the decision to brutally suppress the Nika riots.
- Although she was not elected President of Argentina, Evita Peron (1919-1952) is often thought of as that country's "spiritual leader."
- Catherine the Great was born Sophie Friederike Auguste von Anhalt-Zerbst-Dornburg in what was, at the time, Prussia. She changed her name when she became a member of the Russian Orthodox Church in 1744.
- Just like an Egyptian pharaoh, Hatshepsut had an elaborate mortuary temple built for her deified self. Hatshepsut's temple is located near the village of Deir el-Bahari.
- Argentine President Juan Peron's second wife, Isabel, was sworn in as President of Argentina when he died in 1974. Cristina Fernandez de Kirchner, though was the first woman *elected* as President of Argentina in 2007.
- Joan of Arc (1412-1431) was born a peasant and was never an official ruler, but she did rally the French against the English in the Hundred Years' War. After Joan was captured and burned at the stake, she was proclaimed a saint and heroine of the French people.
- Lili'uokalani was the second ruler of the independent Hawaiian Kingdom and its only female ruler from 1891 to 1893.
- Hatshepsut used the masculine title of "king" in official documents. In art, she is depicted wearing the "false beard" and

hold the crook and flail, which were all symbols of kingship in ancient Egypt.

- Elizabeth I was one of Henry VIII's children and the Queen of England from 1588 to 1603. Often referred to as the "Virgin Queen" because she never married, Elizabeth was the primary force behind England's exploration and colonization of North America.
- Catherine the Great came to power when she overthrew her husband, Peter III. He was arrested and forced to abdicate the throne in 1762 and died shortly thereafter under circumstances that still aren't clear.
- Eleanor of Aquitaine (1122-1204) was the queen of both England and France at different points in her life. She notably took part in the ill-fated Second Crusade (1147-1150).

THE WORLD WARS WERE ALSO ABOUT MONEY

The world wars were caused by several factors: nationalism, political extremism, and a desire for more land are definitely at the top of the list. The goal here isn't to argue about or revisit any of that—you may have been through all that in your high school or college history courses. Not to mention, the History Channel shows that stuff non-stop! No, this is a trivia book, so the goal is to learn a few new things and have some fun in the process.

So, let's talk about some of the economic aspects of World War I and World War II.

Economics played a major role in how and why both wars happened as well as their results. For instance, Russia had no business getting involved in World War I because its people were poor and starving. Once Russia made the fateful decision to enter World War I on the Allies side, it led to its economic collapse and a revolution that ushered in the world's first experiment with the political and economic system of communism.

And World War II probably wouldn't have happened if Germany wasn't hit with the economic crippling process of the hyperinflation of 1921 to 1923 and then the double whammy of the Great Depression, which hit in 1929.

It all paved the way for Hitler to come to power and as they say, "the rest is history."

Random Facts:

- The need to acquire and keep colonies was driven by economics. From 1870 until the start of World War I in 1914, 35% of all British exports went to their colonies.
- Inflation is defined as a sustained increase in the prices of commodities, while hyperinflation is defined as a 50% or more increase. In Germany, inflation peaked at nearly 30,000% in 1923!
- "Autarky" is when a country becomes economically self-sufficient. The Soviet Union and Nazi Germany attempted to become autarkic before World War II.
- Before World War I, most of the major countries involved were part of the economic system known as the "gold standard" or "classical gold standard." Under the system, a country's paper money was completely backed by the gold held in its possession.
- "Operation Fish" was the codename of an Allied operation to physically transfer the gold bullion reserves from England and occupied Europe to Canada and the United States.
- Under the Lend-Lease Act of 1941, the United States gave $50.6 billion in aid to the United Kingdom and United Soviet Socialist Republics until August 21, 1945.
- For its role in World War I, Germany was forced to pay France 132 billion gold marks in reparations.
- During the 1930s, Soviet dictator Joseph Stalin introduced "Five Year Plans" to modernize and industrialize the Soviet Union and to collectivize its agriculture.
- Although Britain was technically one of the "winners" of World War I, it lost nearly one-quarter of its overseas investments and it was the beginning of the end of its once-lucrative empire.

- In 1996, the American Undersecretary of Commerce, Stuart Eizenstat, testified in front of the U.S. Congress that neutral countries such as Switzerland served as a banker for the Axis Powers. The testimony stated that gold and money the Nazis took from conquered governments as well as individuals was funneled through Swiss banks.
- Germany's cycle of hyperinflation ended when the government introduced the Rentenmark as the currency in 1923. It was backed by real estate, with one million Reichsmarks equaling one Rentenmark.
- As World War II was ending in 1944, a new global economic system known as the "Bretton Woods" system was introduced. It was a modified gold standard that lasted until 1976.
- As with Word War I, despite being on the "winning' side of World War II, Britain was one of the bigger economic losers. The British lost most of their colonies, incurred $20 billion debt, and were unable to get the Bretton Woods system based on the pound instead of the dollar.
- "Operation Menace" was the codename of a September 23-25, 1940 raid by the British Navy and Free French forces to capture the city of Dakar, French West Africa, and the Belgian and Polish gold that was being held by the Vichy French in the city. The Vichy French were able to move the gold to safety and also won the battle over the Allies which was very embarrassing for the Allies.
- American President Franklin Delano Roosevelt ordered the confiscation of the nation's gold supply on April 5, 1933.
- Before World War I, Imperial Russia had many loans with France. After the communists came to power in Russia in 1917, they defaulted on the previous Russian government's loan commitments.
- In addition to the high amount of monetary reparations Germany

was forced to pay after World War I, its 16 billion marks in overseas assets were also seized.

- When Germany invaded Norway in April 1940, the Norwegian royal family fled with most of the country's gold to England.
- The American ability to out produce the enemy proved to be as much of a factor to win World War II as anything. For example, after the U.S. entered the war on the Allies' side in 1941, it produced more than 11 million rifles, compared to just over 8.5 produced by all of the Axis Powers for the entire war.
- Despite "losing" World War II, Japan and West Germany emerged in the 1960s to become the leading economies in their regions and among the largest and most powerful economies in the world.

THE NOT-SO-GLORIOUS DEATH OF FREDERICK BARBAROSSA

Few people influenced the course of medieval European history more than Frederick I (ruled 1155-1190), the Holy Roman Emperor, better known as Frederick Barbarossa. Frederick was a truly ambitious man, becoming the Duke of Swabia, the King of Burgundy, King of the Romans, and the King of Italy before rolling all of those titles into one to become the "Emperor of Rome," which was essentially Germany, Italy, and some other territories.

Frederick spent his entire life fighting and conquering. After subduing central Europe and placing it under his rule, he traveled to the Holy Land to fight in the Second Crusade. He returned to Europe for a time but was also eager for the next adventure and/or war.

Although he had effectively placated central Europe, the Crusades were still raging in the Holy Land, so Barbarossa headed south, which is where he met his tragic end.

But Frederick Barbarossa didn't die in a glorious battle during the Third Crusade, he died *on his way* to the Third Crusade. The details of what happened aren't exactly clear, but what is known is that he was attempting to cross the Saleph River in what is today known as modern Turkey when he drowned.

The most common explanation is that he simply fell off his horse as he was crossing the river and was unable to swim due to the weight of his armor.

Random Facts:

- "Barbarossa" is Italian for "red beard." He was known as "Rotbart" in German.
- The "King of the Romans" was essentially the King of Germany. Throughout the Middle Ages, Europeans in the West and East continued to use the titles and symbolism of Rome, although it was in name only.
- Although the "King of the Romans" had absolute power over his realm, it was an elected office. Frederick was elected by the royal electors (princes of the realm) and crowned on March 9, 1152.
- The assembly of the German princes to elect the Emperor was known as the *hoftag*.
- Frederick married Adelaide of Vohburg, the Duchess of Swabia, in 1147. The childless and loveless marriage was annulled by Pope Eugene III in 1153.
- Frederick's father was Frederick II, Duke of Swabia, so he inherited that position when his father died in 1147.
- Frederick began his six military campaigns in Italy in 1154. The intent was to subdue the country, become its king, and also be crowned the Holy Roman Emperor by the pope.
- Pope Hadrian IV crowned Frederick I as the Holy Roman Emperor on June 18, 1155, in St. Peter's Basilica in Rome.
- After Barbarossa's rule, the title of Holy Roman Emperor was also held in conjunction with the "King of Italy" and the "King of Germany/Romans" until the modern period.
- Barbarossa was a member of the powerful Hohenstaufen Dynasty. Members of the dynasty ruled several different principalities, and the Holy Roman Empire, well into the late 13th century.

- Frederick married Beatrice I, the Duchess of Burgundy, on June 9, 1156. The couple had 11 children!
- Barbarossa's Italian campaigns ended when he lost the Battle of Legnano to the Lombard League in 1176.
- Due to his connection to Burgundy through his wife Beatrice, and his recognition of the Burgundian League, Barbarossa was crowned as King of Burgundy at Arles (in present-day France) in 1178.
- Frederick embarked on one final campaign in Italy from 1184-1186. The campaign took place after the new pope, Urban III, opposed Barbarossa.
- The Third Crusade (1189-1192) was a success as far as the crusaders were able to keep their lands in the Levant and gained Cyprus, although they were unable to retake Jerusalem from the Muslims.
- The Third Crusade marked a general period of peace in Europe, as Henry II of England and Philip II of France ended their war to align against the Muslims. The Kingdom of Hungary also joined the crusade, although the Byzantine Empire refused the crusaders' passage through their lands.
- Although Barbarossa's death by falling from his horse is the most repeated version, three other versions have him drowning as he swam in the river.
- Frederick's army was allowed to pass freely with his army by the Turkish Sultan Kilij Arslan II, who ruled that portion of Anatolia (Turkey).
- Barbarossa's remains were interred in three different churches. His flesh went to the Church of St. Peter in Antioch, his bones were buried in the Cathedral of Tyre in Lebanon, and his heart and viscera were interred in St. Paul's Church in Tarsus.

- A modern monument was installed by the Turkish government to mark the spot of Barbarossa's demise. There was also once a statue in the location, but it was stolen.

FORGED IN IRON

Modern historians and archaeologists like to subdivide and categorize world history into different periods, and one of the ways they do that is by considering the type of tools and metals humans used. For most of human history, we have used stone tools, so therefore, the "Stone Age" encompassed history until about 3,300 BCE. After that time, humans in most of Asia and Europe began using bronze tools so the world entered the "Bronze Age."

The Bronze Age was marked by powerful civilizations in Eurasia, especially the Near East. The Bronze Age was the time of ancient Egypt's glory, the kingdoms of Mesopotamia, the Hittites, the Minoans, and the Mycenaean's. The Bronze Age system of the Near East collapsed around 1,200 BCE when wave after wave of human migrations and invasions overwhelmed many of the kingdoms. The invaders became known as the "Sea Peoples," and they helped usher in the Iron Age.

The Iron Age began in the Near East after the Bronze Age collapse and lasted until the 7th or 6th century and at other times in Europe and Asia.

And this is where things get a little tricky.

Most of Africa never experienced a Bronze Age and entered the Iron Age much later than the rest of the world. While the Americas did have advanced cultures (Maya, Aztecs, Incas, etc.), they had very few bronze tools and no iron tools.

The Iron Age only lasted a couple of hundred years in most places, although the precise point at which it ended is open to debate. In Europe, the Roman Empire is often the terminal point, while the Achaemenid Empire (500's BCE) is for the Near East and Central Asia. The emergence of the Mauryan Empire (300s BCE) in India is often seen as the end of the Bronze Age on the subcontinent, and in East Asia, it happened slightly later.

Random Facts:

- "Iron Age" refers specifically to the metallurgy of iron and other metals for tools and weapons, otherwise known as "ferrous metallurgy."
- Iron-working didn't play a dominant role in ancient China, so it has traditionally not been associated with the three age paradigm. Sometimes, though, its Iron Age is listed as taking place from 500 to 100 BCE.
- After the Iron Age, world history is categorized by its "historical periods."
- The term "Sea Peoples" was taken from translations of Egyptian texts. The Kingdom of Egypt survived repeated attacks (1276-1178 BCE) , which is how modern scholars know about the enigmatic peoples.
- The Sea Peoples were several different tribes, many of which never traveled by sea, and who were only occasionally aligned.
- The Moche and Inca peoples of South America developed bronze but not iron-working.
- The production of iron took place very gradually. It began with the occasional working of naturally occurring iron before full-scale smelting took place. The Hittites were among the earliest of the Bronze Age cultures to produced iron weapons, which is ironic since their culture was destroyed during the Bronze Age collapse.
- The Sea Peoples invasions took place until about the mid-12th century BCE.
- Iron production began in Korea in the 2nd century BCE. and a little later in Japan.
- When the Nubians ruled Egypt in the 7th and early 6th centuries

BCE, they learned the secrets of iron-working. After they were driven back south by the Assyrians, the Nubians disseminated iron-working knowledge and are believed to have been a major factor in the spread of iron-working through sub-Saharan Africa.

- To make iron tools and weapons, the metal has to be extracted from oxidized iron ores. This can only be done with extremely high temperatures that Bronze Age kilns were not capable of reaching.
- The Hallstatt Culture of Western Europe lasted from about 1,200 to 500 BCE. The culture was in the Late Bronze age until about 800 BCE and then the Iron Age until its end.
- The Sea Peoples and other migratory tribes in the Late Bronze Age primarily originated in Europe and are believed to have been mainly of Indo-European origins.
- Although it was once believed that the Sea Peoples gain their advantage primarily because they wielded iron weapons, scholars now believe that a combination of factors led to their success and initial movements into the eastern Mediterranean Basin.
- Archaeological evidence shows that the Nok Culture of Nigeria had early iron-working technology by 550 BCE, but the culture disappeared only about 50 years later.
- A mystery of Iron Age Britain is the existence of stone structures known as "fogus." Some have suggested they were used as granaries.
- The Romans knew Austria as "Noricum." It was important to them as a source of iron ore deposits.
- The Egyptian sources list the following names of Sea Peoples tribes: Ekwesh, Luka, Teresh, Shekelesh, Danuna, Weshesh, Peleset, and Shardana. Many of their names are associated with geographic locations. For example, Shardana is associated with the island of Sardinia and the Peleset became the Philistines.

- The legendary city of Troy was destroyed during the Sea Peoples' invasions. It was the seventh Troy built at that location.
- The ancient city of Ugarit was destroyed during the Sea Peoples invasions around 1,200 BCE and although the Hittites were an inland empire, for the most part, the Phrygians dealt a deadly blow against them by invading overland from the north.

CHAPTER 5:

Potpourri - All Rolled Into One

THE SEVEN WONDERS OF THE ANCIENT WORLD

You've no doubt heard the term "Seven Wonders of the World," but have you considered what places are on the list or how the list was compiled? How many sites of the original Seven Wonders of the Ancient World can you name? If you can't name any, or only one or two, don't feel bad. Most people don't know the list, which is partly because only one of the seven original monuments still stands.

So, what are the Seven Wonders of the Ancient World and how did the list begin?

Large-scale monuments were built long before the ancient Greeks came on the scene of world history, but it was the Greeks who decided to classify monuments and buildings according to their importance.

Alexander the Great's conquests brought the Greeks of the Hellenistic Era into direct contact with the temples, monuments, and pyramids of the Near East, which ignited talk about the greatest sites of the world that were "must-see" locations.

The numerical value of the number seven appears to have long been significant as evidenced by other groupings such as the Seven Deadly

Sins, the Seven Sages, and the Seven Daughters of Atlas, to name a few.

The entries on the Seven Wonders of the Ancient World list fluctuated throughout history until it was finally codified during the Renaissance. The seven monuments are the Great Pyramids of Giza, Egypt; the Lighthouse of Alexandria, Egypt; the Hanging Gardens of Babylon (Nineveh), Mesopotamia (Modern Iraq); the Temple of Artemis at Ephesus, Anatolia (Modern Turkey); the Statue of Zeus in Olympia, Greece; the Mausoleum of Halicarnassus and the Colossus of Rhodes, Greece.

Only the Great Pyramids of Giza still stand as a testament to the list and its builders.

Random Facts:

- The Great Pyramids of Giza are the oldest of all the monuments, having been built around 2,500 BCE. Khufu's Pyramid (*the* Great Pyramid), is also taller and covers more area than the other wonders.
- The Lighthouse of Alexandria is Egypt's second entry on the list, although it was built more than 2,000 years later, during the reign of Ptolemy II (ruled 284-246 BCE). The Lighthouse was located on the Pharos Island in Alexandria Harbor, serving as a beacon to travelers and as a customs control for those entering and leaving Egypt.
- The Colossus of Rhodes was designed by an architect named Chares of Lindos to commemorate the small island nation's victory over a Macedonian general named Demetrius. Construction began in 292 BCE and was completed in 280. It was 108 feet tall, made of brass and iron, and stood on a marble pedestal.
- It is often believed that the Great Wall of China is one of the Seven Wonders of the Ancient World, but the Greeks had only very limited knowledge of China.
- The Lighthouse suffered from earthquakes and saltwater erosion throughout the Middle Ages before what was left of it was converted into a fort in 1480.
- The Hanging Gardens of Babylon is the second-oldest entry, having been built in the 7th or 6th century BCE.
- The Mausoleum of Halicarnassus was built for the body of Mausolus, a satrap (provincial governor) in the Persian Empire in the 4th century BCE.
- Medieval versions of the Seven Wonders of the Ancient World

often had a biblical theme. Noah's Ark and the Solomonic Temple in Jerusalem were often at the top of the list.

- The Statue of Zeus was a seated statue of the god made of gold and ivory that stood 41 feet high. It was constructed from 466 to 435 BCE.
- The Temple of Artemis was built in the mid-6th century BCE for the Greek goddesses Artemis (Roman Diana). The Temple was the victim of arson in 356 BCE, but it was rebuilt later that century.
- Modern scholar Stephanie Dalley argued that the Hanging Gardens of Babylon existed, but that they were located to the north in the Assyrian city of Nineveh and were probably built during the reign of the Assyrian King Sennacherib (704-681 BCE).
- The 1st century CE Roman-Jewish historian, Josephus, wrote that the light from the Lighthouse of Alexandria could be seen from more than 30 miles away. The light was produced by fires, but modern scholars believe it was amplified through mirror like structures.
- The Statue of Liberty is about the same height as the Colossus of Rhodes. The title of the poem, "The New Colossus," inscribed on the Statue of Liberty is a reference to the Wonder of the World.
- The three Great Pyramids are often collectively considered one of the Seven Wonders, although many list Khufu's Pyramid as the specific Wonder. The other two pyramids next to Khufu's were Khafre's and Menkaure's.
- The Statue of Zeus survived until the 5th century CE. It is believed to have been brought to Constantinople where it was destroyed in a fire.
- The Mausoleum had the second-longest lifespan of the Wonders and the longest of those now lost. It is believed that a series of earthquakes reduced the structure to rubble by 1404.

- Although the Great Pyramids are still intact, they have been damaged throughout the millennia. The Great Pyramid was once encased in white limestone, but today only the top is still capped in limestone.
- Medieval versions of the Seven Wonders of the Ancient World often had a biblical theme. Noah's Ark and the Solomonic Temple in Jerusalem were often at the top of the list.
- The date of the destruction of the Hanging Gardens remains a mystery. If the Gardens were actually in Nineveh, then they were probably destroyed when the city was sacked by the Medes and Neo-Babylonians in 612 BCE.

LEARNING TO FLY

Probably since the Stone Age, humans have looked to the skies and wondered, "what if?" The thought was enough to inspire myths about humans flying, such as the Greek myth of Icarus. According to the myth, Icarus and his father made wings of wax that allowed them to fly and to escape a dungeon, but Icarus flew too close to the sun and died.

The myth of Icarus is perhaps more allegory than anything, but it represents one of humanity's first theoretical approaches to flight.

Later, Chinese scientists drew up theoretical sketches of flying machines and so too did medieval Arabs and Europeans. Leonardo Da Vinci (1452-1519) is known today for drawing up sketches of various gliders and flying machines, although none influenced the first flight.

Hot air balloons were the first vehicles to bring people into the skies in the 1700s, and by the 1800s, advances in technology allowed scientists and engineers to take the next step to motor-propelled airplanes.

English engineer Sir George Cayley (1773-1857) wrote about the theoretical possibility of heavier than air flying vehicles, and before too long, Orville and Wilbur Wright read his ideas and decided to begin some of experiments of their own.

After a series of failed experiments, the Wright Brothers finally flew the first airplane on the desolate dunes of Kittyhawk, North Carolina on December 17, 1903. The plane only went 120 feet, 12 feet off the ground, but it was the most important flight in history.

No doubt, Icarus would've been proud.

Random Facts:

- The Wright Brothers only had high school educations. They were self-taught engineers and scientists who learned everything they knew from their bicycle shop in Dayton, Ohio.
- The first known hot air balloon flight was undertaken by Brazilian priest Bartolomeu de Gusmão on August 8, 1709, in Lisbon, Portugal. It flew approximately 1.5 miles but it was an unmanned balloon.
- Cayley's is credited with laying the proper theoretical framework behind "heavier than air" flight. His ideas were published in numerous journals, and for that reason, he is credited with being the "father of flight."
- There are numerous claims to successful heavier than air flight before the Wright Brothers, including a boy who flew in a plane designed by Cayley in 1849. Because none of those flights were documented or witnessed by others, the Wright Brothers have the honor of being the "first in flight."
- Kites work on many of the same principles of flight as gliders. The Chinese Emperor Wenxuan is said to have launched several prisoners from a tower in kites. All but one of them died.
- The first manned air balloon flight was done by Frenchman Jean-Francois Pilatre de Rozier on September 19, 1783, at the Palace of Versailles in France. It was a tethered flight. Rozier also did the first untethered, manned balloon flight on November 21, 1783 with this flight achieving 5.5 miles.
- The technical name for a lighter than air aircraft, which includes balloons and dirigibles, is "aerostat."
- The Wright Brothers initially contacted Henry Ford to build the engine for their airplane, but he thought the project was doomed to fail so they had to build their own.

- The medieval Arab scientist Abbas Ibn Firnas (809-887 CE) claimed to have flown briefly in a winged glider that had feathers. Although there's no corroborating source to the claim, Firnas was known to be quite a scholar so it's more than possible.
- Credit for the first controlled manned glider flight goes to Otto Lilenthal. He completed the flight in front of witnesses in 1891 in Potsdam, Germany.
- The Wright Brothers' first flight was documented in a photograph. Wilbur was the pilot.
- Da Vinci drew an early parachute design that was pyramidal in shape, although other designs of parachutes were being drawn around the same time. There is no known parachute, though, from the Renaissance.
- The concept of a helicopter has existed since 400 BCE. From that time on, the Chinese had a small toy known as a "bamboo dragonfly" that operated under the same principles as a helicopter.
- Gustave Whitehead (1874-1927) is an engineer who claims to have beat the Wright Brothers in flight. He claims to have first flown his airplane in 1901 in Connecticut.
- An airship or dirigible is a powered, lighter than air, aircraft. The first successful airship flight was done by Henri Giffard for 15 miles in France on September 24, 1852.
- German aristocrat Ferdinand von Zeppelin (1838-1917) was responsible for inventing a rigid outer frame on airships. The innovation allowed airships to fly across the Atlantic Ocean.
- Samuel Pierpont Langley (1834-1906) was another early aviation pioneer. He flew the first *unpiloted*, heavier than air plane on May 6, 1896.
- Frenchman Louis-Sebastian Lenormand (1757-1837) made the first

parachute jump on December 26, 1783, when he jumped from a tower in Montpellier, France.

- Octave Chanute (1832-1910) was another early aviation pioneer. His stacked wing design was crucial in the success of early heavier than air planes.
- The Wright Brothers were as successful businessmen as they were scientists. They patented and marketed their invention and spent several years suing their competitors.

LOSING THESE GAMES OFTEN MEANT DEATH

We've examined sports violence in recent times in different sections of this book, so now let's go back in time to look at a couple of sports where the death of the athletes was accepted, or even promoted.

The Romans loved a variety of blood sports they called *munera*, which included "hunts" of wild animals and of course gladiatorial combat. Gladiator games began in the 3rd century BCE and lasted until the 400s CE.

Far across the world from Rome, but around the same time, the different peoples of pre-Columbian America played their own deadly game, known today simply as "the ballgame." The ballgame was played sometime after 1,400 BCE by the Olmecs (in what is now Mexico) and was later played by the Maya, Toltecs, and Aztecs, even after the Spanish conquest in 1519 CE.

Although anthropologists and archaeologists are still learning a lot about the details of the ballgame, it's known that it was played by two teams on courts that varied in size but with the same general layout. The goal was to get a rubber ball through a hoop set high up on a wall. The ballgame was more about losing than winning, though.

The losers were usually sacrificed to the gods!

Random Facts:

- *Venatio* was the Latin/Roman term for large public hunts and the killing of animals. The Romans probably got the idea from the ancient Egyptians and Assyrians, who depicted in their art their kings out hunting lions and other animals.
- Mesoamerican ballgames usually consisted of two teams of seven players on each team.
- Gladiators were generally highly trained prisoners of war. They would engage each other in single combat, but the fights were often part of a day of events that included *venationes*.
- Although Roman *munera*/blood sports and the Mesoamerican ballgame were both violent athletic events, the Roman events were almost entirely secular while the Mesoamerican games were deeply intertwined with religion.
- The first organized hunt spectacle/*venatio* in Rome itself was conducted in 186 BCE.
- Mesoamerican ballgames were played in "ballcourts" that resemble an "I" with the wider parts being the endzone for each team. Scoring was done by either hitting the ball through the opposing team's endzone or by knocking the ball through a ring tethered several feet high in the middle of the court.
- The earliest known depiction source of a Roman gladiatorial is known as the "Campanian Gladiator Frescoes," dated to the 4th century BCE. It is believed that the gladiators volunteered as part of funeral games and fought to the first bloodshed.
- Thousands of ball courts were built from what is now the southwest United States down to Nicaragua. There were about 6,000 in Mexico alone.
- Losers of the Mesoamerican ballgame were almost always

sacrificed in elaborate rituals. Beautiful reliefs from the Maya city of Chichen Itza in the Yucatan of Mexico show the post-game ritual instead of the game.

- Death wasn't a given for the losers of gladiator events. A fallen gladiator could raise a finger to appeal to the crowd and/or the referee for his life. If he fought well enough, they were often given *missio*, a sparing of their life.
- The term "gladiator" is derived from *gladius*, which was the name of the sword used by Roman soldiers. Gladiators used many of the same weapons as soldiers.
- The Mesoamerican ballgame was played with a rubber ball that wasn't filled with air, so it was quite hard and heavy.
- Based on reliefs, anthropologists believe that the players of the Mesoamerican ballgame could only use their hips to move the ball.
- Although rare, female gladiators, "gladiatrix", were not unheard of and were popular in different periods of Roman history. Most appear to have been non-Roman, like their male counterparts. They participated in both single gladiator combat and hunts.
- The Colosseum is often associated with Roman gladiators, but it was built quite late. It was begun by Emperor Vespasian (69-79 CE) and completed in 80 CE by his son, Titus (79-81 CE).
- As many as 11,000 animals were killed in games held by Emperor Trajan (98-117 CE) in 107 CE.
- Because the ballgame was so important, rubber became a vital part of the economy in ancient Mesoamerica. For example, according to the Aztec Codex Mendoza, the southern province of Tochtepec supplied 16,000 rubber balls to the Aztecs as part of their yearly tribute.
- At the height of the Roman blood sports in the early Roman Empire, *munera* and *venatio* would be part of a daylong event.

Hunts would often be the first event, or possibly executions of criminal and/or rebels by animals. Dancing and athletics would take place around lunchtime and then the main event would be gladiatorial combat in the afternoon.

- A modern version of the ballgame called *ulama* is played in the Mexican state of Sinaloa. The losers get to keep their heads in this version!
- The Hohokam and Anasazi of the southwest US are believed to have played a version of the ballgame on an oval court. Archaeologists have identified more than 236 ball courts at 166 sites throughout the southwest.

DOO-WOP AND GREASERS

The 1950s United States is often looked at with fondness by those who lived through it. After all, it was the decade after World War II, when the war vets were coming home and starting families, giving birth to the Baby Boomer generation. It was a time of relative peace and prosperity, but it was also a time of cultural change.

New musical styles were forming and making their way into the mainstream and along with them, new youth cultures.

One of the more important musical styles of the 1950s was "doo-wop."

Doo-wop refers to the early rock and roll style made famous by young Black male musicians in the 1950s. They usually sang a cappella in groups, throwing in plenty of syllables and words that didn't make much sense; words such as "doo-wop."

Doo-wop became a major sensation, due in large part to its crossover appeal to both Black and White youths. Many of the kids buying doo-wop albums and going to doo-wop shows were members of the "greaser" subculture.

Greasers were primarily White and Hispanic working-class youths who adopted a tough look that included: hair greased back with Vaseline or Brylcream, jeans, engineer boots, white t-shirts, and a black leather jacket. Greaser also liked to keep a cigarette behind one of their ears and roll a pack of smokes up in one of the sleeves of their t-shirt.

Although the greaser subculture was more of a style than anything, some greasers were drawn to early street and biker gangs.

Random Facts:

- Although doo-wop was male-dominated, there were some notable female doo-wop groups. The Mellows was the name of a female doo-wop group that recorded several hits during the early 1950s.
- Like most styles of American music, doo-wop has diverse origins. Jazz and early rhythm and blues were some of the most obvious origins, but barbershop quartet music was also a major influence on do-wop.
- It's believed that the term "greaser" was originally meant as an ethnic slur. In the early years, many of the young men in the greaser subculture were Italian, Puerto Rican, and Mexican-American.
- More successful doo-wop groups used instruments when they performed live or in the recording studio, but new groups were a cappella. The extra and made up "doo-wop" syllables doo-wop musicians used served as a substitute for drums.
- The musical, book, and film, *West Side Story* is about two gangs—one White/Anglo, one Puerto Rican—who fought over turf on Manhattan's Upper West Side. Both gangs are usually depicted in the greaser style.
- Doo-wop groups often performed live on street corners.
- Doo-wop didn't immediately die when the 1960s came. One of the biggest doo-wop hits of all time "The Lion Sleeps Tonight" by the Tokens came out in 1961.
- Plenty of girls were also part of the greaser subculture. Greaser girls wore plenty of makeup, big hair, tight pants, and high heels.
- *The Outsiders* was a 1967 novel by S.E. Hinton about greasers in Tulsa, Oklahoma in the early 1960s. The book is said to have been one of the forces behind the so-called "greaser revival" of the 1970s.

- American rock band Sha-Na-Na combined greaser culture and doo-wop in their act during the 1970s. The name of the band was itself a reference to the meaningless syllables common in do-wop. "Yip yip yip yip yip yip yip yip Mum mum mum mum mum mum Get a job, sha na na na, sha na na na na" are the lyrics to the 1957 doo-wop hit "Get a Job" by the Silhouettes.
- After doo-wop's initial surge in popularity, many White groups began forming. Many of the White doo-wop groups were from the East Coast and of Italian-American heritage.
- The 1955 film *Blackboard Jungle* captures a little bit of doo-wop and greaser culture in a way that would probably seem strange to most audiences today.
- The British equivalents of greasers in the 1950s were known as "Teddy Boys." Although the Teddy Boys dressed in a different style to greasers, they often formed gangs and engaged in rebellious activities like their American counterparts.
- In doo-wop's early years, its records were usually on the rhythm-and-blues or "race record" charts and categories. The song "Sh-Boom" by the Chords was one of the earliest doo-wop songs to crossover into the top 10 of the pop charts.
- Although the switchblade knife became associated with greasers in the 1950s, much of it was based on paranoia caused by films like *Blackboard Jungle*. The general paranoia led to legislation that restricted switchblade sales in 1958 federally, and several states followed suit, some even banning them.
- Although doo-wop was dead by the mid-'60s, some of the bands lived on. The Platters, who are best known for their hit "The Great Pretender," changed their style with the times and became even more popular.
- Greasers were considered to have long hair in the 1950s. Most men wore their hair in a "crew cut" style at the time, while

greasers liked to have a little length and comb their hair in a pompadour in the front or a "ducktail" in the back.

- A good doo-wop group featured a range of different vocal sounds, from high (falsetto) to low (bass).
- Besides, Sha Na Na, America's love of doo-wop, the greaser subculture, and the 1950s in general, were seen in other elements of 1970s pop culture with the television series *Happy Days*, in which one of the main characters, "The Fonze," was a greaser. The 1971 musical *Grease* and 1978 film of the same name were also about the 1950s greaser subculture.
- Surfer band The Beach Boys were influenced by doo-wop, among other musical styles. For example, the song "Surfer Girl" was based on "When You Wish Upon a Star" by the doo-wop group Dion and the Belmonts.

SAY THAT AGAIN

The idea of language is something that most of us take for granted and rarely consider. Humans have been using spoken language to communicate for at least 200,000 years, probably longer, and have been employing writing for the last 3,000 years. Language is important on a practical level because it is used not only for mundane, everyday purposes but also as a method for people to express cultural ideas.

Languages all originate in a specific geographic location and their spread throughout the world can be traced geographically.

More than 3.2 billion people in the world—about 46% of the total population—speak an Indo-European language. Indo-European refers to a cultural-linguistic group and is sometimes called a "language family." Most modern European languages are Indo-European as well as Farsi, Hindi, and other languages that are spoken in India. Indo-European languages began with a cultural group in the Eurasian Steppe in the Neolithic Period and then spread west, south, and east through migrations and invasions. In modern times, Europeans brought Indo-European languages to their colonies.

Today, nearly everyone in North America and South America speaks one of four Indo-European languages: English, Spanish, Portuguese, or French.

The Semitic cultural-linguistic group began in the Middle East in the Neolithic Period and has been the dominant language group in that region ever since. Akkadian, Hebrew, and various Canaanite dialects were common in the Bronze Age. Later, as Islam spread throughout the world from the 6th century on, the Semitic language of Arabic spread along with it and is now the primary language of more than 400 million people and is used in religious services by 1.8 billion people.

A similar origin took place in China with the Sinitic family of languages, giving birth to Mandarin Chinese, which has since spread throughout the world.

Random Facts:

- "Linguistic geography" is the proper term for the study of the geographic distribution of languages. The fields of linguistics and geography influence linguistic geography, but most of its experts are linguists.
- English is the most spoken Indo-European language in the world. It is the primary/first language of 370 million people and the second language of 898 million people. Although it ranks third overall as the most widely spoken first language behind Mandarin Chinese and fellow Indo-European language Spanish, the number of second-language speakers makes it the most spoken language overall.
- Languages of the Polynesian language family are the most widely-spoken languages in the South Pacific, which include Hawaiian, Maori, and Samoan.
- The English language's global distribution is largely the result of the dominance of the British Empire in the 1700s and 1800s.
- Arabic originated in what is today Saudi Arabia in the 1st century CE. It was spread forcefully after the birth of Islam in the 7th century CE and is now the primary language in 26 countries covering over 10% of the Earth's surface.
- In addition to facilitating the spread of the English language across the globe, the British Empire also helped to spread other languages. From the mid-1800s to 1880, nearly 200,000 ethnic Chinese subjects of the British migrated to several locations throughout southeast Asia, particularly Singapore and Malaysia.
- Although English and Spanish are the dominant languages in New World countries, indigenous languages are still widely distributed. For example, in Brazil, more than 200 indigenous languages are still

spoken and 60 indigenous languages are still spoken in Canada.

- Languages were spread primarily through warfare and migration in the ancient and medieval periods.
- In addition to being spoken by more people, English is spoken over a wider area and claims more landmass than any other language. It's the primary language in 77 countries, covering more than 23% of the Earth's surface.
- The languages that are descended from the ancient Indo-European language Latin are known as "Romance" languages. French, Spanish, Portuguese, Italian, and Romanian all began as local dialects of Latin but evolved into distinct languages by the early Middle Ages.
- Romance is the largest branch of the Indo-European family. More than 800 million people speak a Romance language as their primary language and Romance language countries and territories cover about 30% of the world's surface.
- The extent of the Russian language's geographic distribution has fluctuated with its imperial ambitions. Non-Russian elites in the Russian Empire before World War II and the Soviet Union after World War II learned Russian as their second language to keep their high social positions.
- The majority of the spread of the Sino-Tibetan language family has been the result of three languages: Sinitic (Chinese), Burmese, and Tibetan. The geographic spread of the Sino-Tibetan languages has been far less extensive—or aggressive— than that of the Indo-European language family.
- The Bantu language family is the largest in terms of numbers of speakers and geographic distribution among sub-Saharan African languages. About 350 million people speak Bantu languages across central and Southern Africa.
- Despite the name, the Indo-Europeans didn't begin populating Europe until about 4,000 BCE. They displaced and eliminated

natives on the continent, which can be seen in modern languages. Basque is a language spoken by about 750,000 people in the Pyrenes region of northwestern Spain and southwestern France: it is the only non-Indo-European language spoken by native Western Europeans.

- You may think of Hungarians as Slavic, but they're not. Hungarians speak Magyar, which is a non-Indo-European language that was brought to central Europe by Magyar nomads in the 9th century CE.
- Although the city of Macau is located in China and most of its inhabitants are ethnic Chinese, Portuguese is the official language along with Chinese. Portugal conquered Macau in the 1500s until it was officially transferred to China in 1999.
- The Polynesian languages were primarily spread through aggressive exploration and conquests from 500 BCE to 1000 CE. By that year Polynesian languages were spoken from Easter Island in the east to the Solomon Islands in the west and from Hawaii down to New Zealand.
- Before the arrival of Europeans, languages in the Uto-Aztecan family were probably the most widely-spoken and geographically distributed in North America.
- Beginning in the mid-1800s, the British distributed millions of Indians and their languages throughout the Empire. Although most of the Indians who moved within the empire were skilled workers and knew English, they continued to speak Hindi and other languages in their shops and homes in Africa, the Caribbean, and southeast Asia.
- South Africa was, and still is, a country of many different languages. In addition to English and the many different native African languages that are spoken there, Afrikaans is spoken by more than ten million people in the country. Afrikaans is a Dutch-derived language that formed in South Africa with Dutch pioneers

in the 1700s.

THE SILENT SCREEN

The idea of films/movies without sound may seem like a pretty difficult concept for many of us to grasp. Dialogue is an important part of any film, especially for films that rely on a well-written, complex plot. Sound effects are also an important aspect of many films.

Can you imagine watching an action film and not hear the sound of gunshots or things exploding? It may be difficult to imagine movies without sound, but that was exactly the reality of the film industry from 1894 to 1929.

That was the era of silent films.

You've probably seen clips of silent films sometime in your life, but you've probably never sat through an entire film. Silent films are so different than today and require an entirely different way of viewing and conceptualizing film that most of us don't have the patience to do so. After all, movies are supposed to be an enjoyable escape, right?

Another reason why you've probably never seen a silent film is that 70% of all silent films have been lost. The films of that era were made with nitrate, which is extremely flammable and doesn't stand up well against the test of time.

But there is no denying that silent films played an extremely important role in the history of pop and film culture in the United States and throughout the world. The very idea of film was a major technological advance that came on the heels of photography, so it needed time to evolve into what it is today.

Random Facts:

- Since there was no dialogue in silent films that could let the audience know the plot's background, intertitles—or title cards—were used. Intertitles were simply text printed on a card that was filmed and placed in important parts of the movie to briefly explain certain situations.
- Acting in silent films required a slightly different skill set than acting in a sound film, or "talkies," as they were known in their early years. Silent film actors had to be more expressive with their hands and face to compensate for the lack of dialogue.
- The highest-grossing silent film of all time is D.W's Griffith's 1915 *Birth of a Nation*. You may find it hard to believe that the Ku Klux Klan were the good guys in that film!
- Thomas Edison is best known for his work and inventions with electricity, but he also had a patent for an early motion picture viewer known as a kinetoscope. Edison later opened film studios in New Jersey and New York.
- Lillian Gish (1893-1993) was one of the best-known actresses of the silent film era. She began her career in 1912 and acted well into the talkie era, making her last appearance in the 1987 film *The Whales of August*.
- Today, "A-list" actors may only do one or two movies a year, but in the silent film era, it wasn't uncommon for some of the top names in the industry to star in a dozen or more films in a year.
- Silent movies were almost always screened with live music. The movie theaters provided the music and musical scores, but by the late 1910s, original scores were often written by the film companies.
- The 1917 silent film *Cleopatra*, starring Theda Bara in the lead role,

only exists in fragments. It was the first film adaption of Shakespeare's plays about the Egyptian queen.

- Eadweard Muybridge (1830-1904) is often thought of as the father of film. He produced a series of short films of horses in motion in 1877 and 1878. The Horse in Motion is a series of cabinet cards by Eadweard Muybridge, including six cards that each show a sequential series of six to twelve "automatic electro-photographs" depicting the movement of a horse.
- As big-budget, epic films such as *Ben-Hur* (1925) and *Birth of the Nation* became more popular, the American film industry moved from the east coast to Hollywood. The early film studios chose Hollywood because the generally sunny, warm weather of southern California allowed consistent shooting of outdoor scenes.
- Most people are familiar with the 1956 *Ten Commandments* starring Charlton Heston, but a 1923 silent version came first. The 1923 version is the tenth-highest grossing silent film of all time.
- As with the transition to color and later high definition, silent films were still being produced into the 1930s as early talking picture films were being produced. *The Jazz Singer* (1927) was the first talkie film, but after its release, the transition to talkies was more gradual than sudden.
- Englishman Charlie Chaplin (1889-1977) got his start in silent films. Although most of Chaplin's career was after the silent era, he is perhaps best known for the silent era character known as "The Tramp," who he played in several films. The Tramp is easily recognizable for his bowler hat, mustache, and cane.
- Although extremely popular at the time, *The Birth of a Nation* was protested by groups such as the NAACP and it was banned in some cities by White mayors. Still, most film critics gave it favorable reviews and it was screened at the Whitehouse for President Woodrow Wilson.

- *The Big Parade* (1925) is the second-highest-grossing silent film of all time.
- In addition to acting in many silent films, Charlie Chaplin also began directing during the silent film era. His 1925 film *The Gold Rush* is the fifth highest-grossing silent film of all time.
- The 1927 German silent film *Metropolis,* was one of the first big-budget, feature-length science fiction films produced. It took nearly two years to make the film, which became famous for its pioneering special effects, namely the use of miniatures to portray the futuristic city.
- In addition to most of the films of the silent era being lost, the vast majority of film scores were also lost by the mid-20th century.
- Roscoe "Fatty" Arbuckle (1887-1933) was a comedic acting icon of the silent era, who like Charlie Chaplin was known for his body humor. Arbuckle was accused and tried for the murder of a woman in 1921, and although he was ultimately acquitted, his acting career was ruined.
- Through what is known as the process of tinting and toning, many silent-era films were in color. Because the colorization process interfered with the process of adding sound to film, early sound films had to be in black and white.
- In Japan during the silent era, theaters had a narrator called a *benshi*. Besides describing the background of the film for the audience, the *benshi* also translated the intertitles from English to Japanese for the audience.

MEDICINE IN THE ANCIENT WORLD

Many people believe that all forms of science "began" in the 1700s during the Age of Enlightenment. Although it's true that modern science as we know it was born in that era, science is more of a process than anything, and it began thousands of years ago when the cavemen learned how to make better tools.

Early science also includes when our hunter and gatherer ancestors used certain herbs and plants for medicinal purposes.

The earliest documented medical texts come from Egypt and Babylon, where medical prescriptions were given to patients along with plenty of magical spells. For the people of ancient Egypt and Mesopotamia, science was heavily intertwined with religion and what we know as the scientific process had yet to be used, but they were on their way.

Farther to the east, medical science was also practiced in India and China. A man named Sushruta wrote a medical text in the 6th century BCE that details early surgical methods in India and China prescriptions and drugs began being cataloged and documented as early as 1,100 BCE.

But it was the Greeks who applied the scientific method to previous medical knowledge. The Greeks also systematized the medical profession and added the system of ethics to it known at the "Hippocratic Oath," which is still used today around the world.

Although the Greek scientist Hippocrates (c. 460-370 BCE) is often called the "Father of Medicine" and he did start an ancient medical school, the oath itself may have been attributed to him later due to his fame.

Random Facts:

- The process of mummification was crucial to the Egyptian understanding of human physiology. The embalmers removed the liver, lungs, stomach, and intestines of the deceased and placed them in jars, while the brain was removed by a rod piece by piece and then discarded.
- In ancient Indian medicine, the blood vessels were known as *nadis*. They were believed to be how spiritual energy was transferred throughout the body and knowledge of them played an important part of the yogic practices of Hinduism.
- One of the earliest known Mesopotamian physicians was a man named Esagil-kin-apli. He wrote a medical text known as *The Diagnostic Handbook* during the reign of Adad-apla-Iddina of Borsippa (1,067-1,046 BCE).
- The Greek-Roman Galen (129-200) is believed to have been one of the greatest physicians and philosophers of the ancient world. Galen traveled extensively but lived primarily in Alexandria, Egypt. Galen was known for performing vivisections on many animals to learn what were at the times the secrets of mammalian biology.
- The peoples of the Pre-Columbian Americas were adept at herb lore, but there is also evidence they practiced some advanced surgery. The Spanish noted that the Aztecs had advanced knowledge of human biology and had names for most of the major organs.
- The people of the Indus Valley Civilization in India (3,200-1,900 BCE) had advanced knowledge of dentistry. The first teeth drilling may have taken place in India around 7,000 BCE.
- The "House of Life" was the ancient Egyptian equivalent of a medical school.

- In traditional Chinese medicine, it's believed that illness is caused by a disruption of the "*qi*" or vital force.
- In addition to influences from earlier cultures, Greek medicine was based on the idea that the human body is comprised of four chemical systems known as "humors": blood, yellow bile, black bile, and phlegm. They believed that illness was usually caused by a disproportion of the humors.
- The *Sushruta Samhita* is a medical text believed to have been written by Sushruta. The ancient Sanskrit word for medicine and the medical practice is "*ayurveda*."
- Imhotep was an ancient Egyptian scientist who is best known for designing King Zoser's "step pyramid" in the early to mid-3rd millennium BCE. He was also a physician and became associated with the Greek god of medicine, Asclepius.
- The oldest extant fragments of the Hippocratic Oath are dated to 275 CE.
- Aztec physicians knew how to set broken bones of their warriors and used sutures instead of cauterization.
- The first doctor to use anesthesia in China—and probably the world—was Hua Tao (140-208 CE).
- Although the Egyptians recognized the brain as a vital part of a properly-functioning body, they believed that emotions and thought came from the heart.
- The *caduceus* is a symbol of Hermes that has become the modern symbol of medicine. The god Asclepius, though, was symbolized by the "Rod of Asclepius," which was a single stick with a long snake entwined on it.
- The Romans adopted Greek medicine generally but introduced the first hospitals to the world, known as a *valetudinarium*.
- Ancient Egyptian physicians rarely practiced medicine full-time and usually worked in other fields, particularly law.

- “Trepanning” is the term for boring a skull in a person’s head to relieve pressure or alleviate some perceived disease or ailment. The earliest archaeological evidence of trepanning dates back to 6,500 BCE in France.

BULLFIGHTING, ANCIENT AND MODERN

Bullfighting is a sport that people in most parts of the world have a difficult time wrapping their heads around. Many see it as cruel and pointless and something that should be done away with altogether. But to millions of people in Spain and Latin America, it's a part of their culture. And in fact, it's an ancient European tradition that many of us share.

The first evidence of bullfighting comes from ancient Crete around 1,500 BCE, where the Minoans created beautiful frescoes of athletes leaping over bulls. Unfortunately, no written texts accompany these works of art. Even if they did, it wouldn't matter, because the language of the Minoans is yet to be deciphered, so we don't know the exact context of these events. They could have been part of athletic competition, a religious ceremony, or a combination of both.

Later, the Romans hunted bulls and other animals in their stadiums for sport.

By the Middle Ages, bullfighting became a popular pastime and sport in Spain and Portugal among both Christians and Muslims. The bulls were respected for their strength and virility, and any man who could kill one was also respected.

The tradition also spread north to France and eventually to the Americas with Spanish and Portuguese colonists. Today, bullfighting is a big money business and although animal rights groups have made great gains in getting it banned in some places, it continues to be popular in many regions of France, Spain, and Latin America.

Random Facts:

- A Spanish-style bullfight is a highly ritualized affair with many different people involved over three stages: the *tercio de varas*, the *tercio de banderillas*, and the *tercio de muerte*.
- Other than the bull, the *matador*, or bullfighter, is the only athlete involved in all three stages of the fight. He uses a brightly colored cloak in the first stage of the fight to wow the crowd and to assess the abilities of the bull.
- The best example of a Minoan bull-leaping scene is the "Bull Fresco" from the palace of Knossos, Crete.
- Spain's best-selling newspaper, *El País*, prints reviews of bullfights in its sports section.
- Portuguese style bullfighting differs from the Spanish version in a couple of notable ways. First, there are only two major stages in a Portuguese bullfight, and second, the bull is never killed in front of the audience.
- The Plaza de Toros Mexico (Stadium of Mexican Bulls) in Mexico City, Mexico, is the largest bullfighting arena in the world. It seats about 46,000 people.
- The matador is accompanied by two *picadors* in the first stage of a Spanish-style bullfight. The picadors ride horses and lance the bull to weaken it for the matador.
- In the second stage of a Spanish style bullfight, the matador places two large darts called *banderillas* into the mound of muscle on the bull's back.
- Although bullfighting is still quite popular in Mexico, it's banned in the states of Sonora, Guerrero, Coahuila, and Quintana Roo.
- You may find this hard to believe, but China has a version of

bullfighting that mixes it with martial arts. No weapons are used, but the bulls are generally chained to a post to hinder their movement.

- The tradition of Minoan bull-leaping continued in Spain into modern times, with many believing that American rodeo clowns of today are the current successor of that tradition.
- The third and final stage of a Spanish style bullfight is the "episode of death." This is when the matador uses his red cape as the bull passes. The crowd yells "toro, toro" (bull, bull) and the matador thrusts a sword into the bull, ideally killing it quickly.
- Spanish style bullfighting is the most popular style throughout the world.
- The Spanish word for bullfight is *corrida*.
- The top matadors can make about $100,000 per year. They often work a circuit, doing fights in Spain, and then traveling to Latin America. A top matador can fight 30 to 40 times per year.
- The more liberal regions of Catalonia and the Canary Islands of Spain have banned bullfighting.
- Though it's not uncommon for a matador to be injured in a bullfight, it's rare for one to be killed. Spaniard Ivan Fandino was the last major, professional matador to die in a bullfight after he was gored in France in 2017. Although the records aren't precise, it's estimated that over 40 professional matadors have died in the ring since 1700.
- Women have been bullfighting since at least the 1700s, but they were banned from fighting in Spain from the 1930s until 1974.
- As the popularity of bullfighting has decreased overall in Spain, it has increased in southern France. French bullfights are often held in ancient Roman amphitheaters, such as the one at Arles.
- Rafael Sanchez (1841-1900), known to his fans and the public as

"Lagartijo" (the Lizard), is probably the most legendary Spanish bullfighter of all-time. He fought for nearly 30 years and was gored seven times!

- Spaniard Enrique Ponce is the highest-paid matador of all-time and is an ironman in the sport, becoming the first person to have fought in 2,000 corridas. He has fought throughout Europe and Latin America and survived a severe goring in 2014.

WEST, EAST, NORTH, AND SOUTH

Previously in this book, you learned more about the North and South poles than most people know, so let's move on to how the Earth is divided by geographers and cartographers. The Earth is technically a sphere, or a globe, that can be divided into two halves known as "hemispheres." The term hemisphere is from the ancient Greek word meaning "half of a sphere," but there are several hemispheres of the planet.

From a purely scientific standpoint, there are only the Northern and Southern Hemispheres. The Equator, which is the imaginary line determined to be 0° latitude, marks the separation between the northern and southern hemispheres. The two hemispheres are very different in terms of landmass and seasons but not necessarily in culture.

The Southern Hemisphere is about 80% water and contains just over 32% of the Earth's land versus just over 60% and 67% for those same categories in the Northern Hemisphere. Because of that, the Southern Hemisphere has far fewer people than the North and the countries of the South have also had less of an impact on world history.

Perhaps the biggest difference between the Northern and Southern Hemispheres are their seasons. Because of the Earth's rotation around the Sun and the ecliptic plane that it is on, the seasons are opposite in the hemispheres. When it's summer in St. Paul, it's winter in Wellington, and when its spring in Sydney, it's fall in Frankfurt.

The world can also be divided into Eastern and Western hemispheres, although this division is much less scientific or exact. The dividing line for the Eastern and Western hemispheres is the Prime Meridian in Greenwich, United Kingdom.

Although lines of longitude have been used since ancient times, the Prime Meridian wasn't adopted until 1884. Everything east of the Prime

Meridian and west of the 180° meridian/longitude is considered the Eastern Hemisphere, while the other half is the Western Hemisphere.

The 180° meridian is in the middle of the South Pacific.

The Earth is also sometimes divided into Eastern and Western hemispheres that are purely political and cultural but are close to the geographical division of east and west.

Random Facts:

- Australia is the only continent completely within the Southern Hemisphere.
- All of Europe and North America are within the Northern Hemisphere.
- Interestingly, the far eastern tip of Siberia (Russia) is in the Western Hemisphere, but the far eastern tip of the Aleutian Islands (Alaska, United States) is in the Eastern Hemisphere. The U.S. possessions of Guam and the Marianna Islands are also in the Eastern Hemisphere.
- Outside of Australia, the Southern Cone is the most economically prosperous in the Southern Hemisphere. The Southern Cone includes the countries of Argentina, Chile, and Uruguay, and occasionally southern Brazil and Paraguay.
- Mount Aconcagua has the distinction of being the tallest mountain in both the Southern and Western hemispheres. It stands 22,837 feet above sea level in the Argentine Andes.
- Over 6.5 billion people live in the Northern Hemisphere, which is about 90% of the world's population. Only about 800 million people live in the Southern Hemisphere.
- Although Greenland is entirely within the Western Hemisphere and closer to Canada than Europe, it's part of Denmark, which is in the Eastern Hemisphere. Despite Greenland's proximity to North America, it has always been more closely aligned to Europe due to Viking history.
- In the Southern Hemisphere, hurricanes are called cyclones and although they tend to behave the same way, for the most part, they move clockwise as opposed to counterclockwise, as they do in the Northern Hemisphere. The reason for this is due to the

Coriolis force, which causes moving objects to be deflected to the right in the Northern Hemisphere and to the left in the Southern Hemisphere.

- Since China and India are in the Eastern Hemisphere, it shouldn't be a surprise that more than 82% of the Earth's population is in the East.
- You may be surprised to learn that Portuguese is the most widely-spoken language in the Southern Hemisphere. Besides more than 200 million Brazilians speaking Portuguese as their primary language, it is also the primary language of several African countries, including Angola and Mozambique.
- The Western and Eastern hemispheres were once frequently referred to be their Latin derived terms, "Occidental" and "Oriental," respectively. The terms are considered somewhat archaic but are still used in some places, such as academia. For example, The Oriental Institute of The University of Chicago studies the cultures of the ancient Near East.
- Different stars and constellations are more visible, or not visible at all, depending upon if you're in the Northern Hemisphere or Southern Hemisphere. Polaris (the North Star), the Big Dipper, and the Little Dipper can only be seen in the Northern Hemisphere. The Southern Cross is visible throughout the year in the Southern Hemisphere but is only visible in the Northern Hemisphere near the Tropic of Cancer during the winter and spring for brief periods of the day.
- The Republic of Kiribati is the only country to have land in all four hemispheres. Kiribati is a collection of 32 atolls and one raised island in the South Pacific.
- The Amazon River marks the approximate division between the Northern and Southern hemispheres in the Americas.
- The designation of "East" and "West" was often muddled during

the Cold War. Most of Asia, which is in the geographical Eastern Hemisphere, sided with the United States and the "West," while many of the "Eastern" nations, such as Hungary and Poland, were traditionally part of Western Civilization/culture.

- Because the Southern Hemisphere has much more water, its temperatures are more moderate than in the Northern Hemisphere.
- The Galapagos Islands in the South Pacific is the geographical center of the Western Hemisphere, while the Eastern Hemisphere's center is in the Indian Ocean west of Indonesia.
- The geographical center of all landmass on the Earth was once thought to be Khufu's Great Pyramid in Giza, Egypt. Many thought that the discovery was highly meaningful until a new study was conducted in 1973 that put the geographical center in Turkey.
- The globe has also been divided by some experts into a "Land Hemisphere" and a "Water Hemisphere." The Land Hemisphere includes all of North America, Europe, and Africa, and most of Asia and South America. The Water Hemisphere includes the rest of the planet, with Australia being the only continent completely in it.
- The Tropic of Cancer is the circle of latitude located at about 23° north latitude. It is the most northerly latitude where the Sun is directly overhead. The Tropic of Capricorn in the Southern Hemisphere is the Tropic of Cancer's counterpart, located at 23° south latitude.

IT ALL STARTED WITH VAUDEVILLE

Television and film haven't been around very long when you think about it. TV has been affordable and available for under 100 years and film became popular just over 100 years ago, and both of those media took time to develop.

So, what did people do for entertainment before then?

Entertainment in the 1800s was all about live acts. Circuses, Old West shows, and "medicine shows" were all forms of popular, live entertainment in the 1800s, but the most popular and impactful were the "vaudeville shows."

The exact origin of the term "vaudeville" is unknown, other than it came from France. What it came to mean in the United States and Canada in the late 1800s was a live variety show. A vaudeville show would feature a bevy of diverse acts, including jugglers, clowns, comedians and sketch comedy, minstrels, strongmen, and singers.

Vaudeville and its related live entertainment shows, such as American burlesque, were extremely popular well into the 1900s before sound could be applied to film.

But in the end, it was film that spelled the end of vaudeville. Vaudeville shows often incorporated films into their acts, but by the mid-1930s most people found that it was much easier just to go to a movie house. Many of the notable vaudeville actors, such as Abbott and Costello, transitioned from vaudeville to film and television, ensuring that vaudeville would be relegated to the dustbin of entertainment history.

With that said, modern film and television owe a debt of gratitude to vaudeville for blazing the entertainment trails.

Random Facts:

- There was no hard rule concerning how many acts a typical vaudeville show had, but it was usually less than ten but more than four or five.
- Most vaudeville shows were family-friendly, allowing women and children to watch. The acts were generally written for a middle-class, middle-America audience.
- Vaudeville shows were performed on theater circuits in mid-size to large cities throughout the United States and Canada. Benjamin Franklin Keith (1846-1914) and Edward Albee (1857-1930) developed theater chains and circuits that standardized vaudeville content and brought the acts to every corner of North America.
- George "Gabby" Hayes is best known for being a sidekick to American Western heroes Hopalong Cassidy and Roy Rogers, but he got his start acting in vaudeville.
- "American burlesque" overlapped vaudeville in terms of its era and somewhat in style, but its content was very different. Although American burlesque featured variety shows with singing and dancing, the acts were often very bawdy complete with plenty of sexual innuendos.
- Minstrel acts, where White performers wore "blackface" makeup, were a common and popular part of any vaudeville show. Minstrel acts preceded vaudeville, peaking in popularity before the American Civil War. Minstrels were gradually incorporated into vaudeville shows, but even in the early 1900s, the idea of blackface was too much for many people as the shows fell out of favor.
- The term "burlesque" is derived from the Italian word "burlesco," which means "jesting" or "joking."

- Koster and Bial's Music Hall in New York City was one of the most famous and important vaudeville theaters. It was the location of the first public showing of a motion picture on April 23, 1896, which ironically spelled the beginning of the end for vaudeville.
- Although vaudeville for the most part stayed away from politics and race—other than minstrel acts, which were considered mainstream at the time—racially segregated seating was enforced in many theaters. Also, language-specific circuits formed to cater to specific ethnic groups: Italian, Yiddish, German, etc.
- American "strip clubs" can trace their origins to American burlesque. One of the most popular burlesque acts, at least for the men in the crowds, was the striptease.
- Although truly an American form of entertainment and primarily popular in the United States and Canada, vaudeville did spread to other countries around the world. Mexico had a thriving vaudeville scene in the early 1920s, with actress Lupe Velez being one of the more notables stars in that country to make the transition to the silver screen.
- The Theatre Owners Booking Association (T.O.B.A.) was an African-American vaudeville circuit in the 1920s. The circuit featured Black actors who played for Black crowds, although the theaters were often owned by Whites.
- The two biggest burlesque circuits in the early 1900s were the Columbia Amusement Company and the Mutual Burlesque Association. Although Columbia had a head start, Mutual ended up lasting longer because it wasn't afraid to push the envelope with progressively more risqué shows.
- Vaudeville performers began their careers in small theaters in small to mid-sized cities. If a performer was talented enough and had a little luck, he or she could hit the "big time" and land a gig

on one of the big circuits. The mecca of vaudeville in the early 1900s was the 1,740 seat Palace Theatre in New York City.

- There have been multiple surges of interest in vaudeville since its demise in the 1930s. Most notable, during the 1970s many sitcoms, such as *Maude* and *Sanford and Son*, featured episodes where the characters performed vaudeville acts.
- The "cabaret" was a style of entertainment popular in Europe during the late 1800s and early 1900s. Like vaudeville, cabaret consisted of a variety of different acts, but they were usually performed in smaller venues, such as bars or lounges. Cabaret also tended to be much more risqué, similar to burlesque.
- Rose Louise Hovik (1911-1970), better known by her stage name, "Gypsy Lee Rose," was a major innovator of the burlesque striptease. An accomplished singer and dancer, Rose incorporated all her talents, and some humor, as she "took it all off for the boys!"
- The 1910s were the high watermark of vaudeville. New York City boasted 48 theaters in 1911, Chicago had 41, and Philadelphia had 37. There were at least 700 vaudeville houses scattered across America by 1920.
- The "revue" was another form of live entertainment that blurred the line between vaudeville and burlesque. Revues were slightly risqué variety shows whose target audiences were a little higher on the socio-economic ladder than a vaudeville crowd.
- Famous New York Mayor Fiorella LaGuardia went after the major burlesque theaters in the late 1930s and early 1940s, driving many into the underground and all but wiping out what was already a declining form of entertainment.

THE SWEET SCIENCE

Slightly ahead of hockey in popularity throughout the world is boxing. Despite being such an immensely popular sport throughout the world, boxing is often maligned as cruel, barbaric, and not a true sport.

Comedian George Carlin once wrote about boxing that, "Boxing is not a sport either. Boxing is a way to beat the shit out of somebody. In that respect, boxing is actually a more sophisticated way of hockey."

But not all intellectuals have agreed with this assessment. British journalist Pierce Egan (1772-1849) famously referred to boxing as the "sweet science" and the moniker has stuck. It's stuck because a good boxer has to perfectly use a combination of athleticism, mental strength, endurance, and some physics to defeat their opponent in a *mono o mono* showdown.

The oldest documentation of organized boxing can be traced back to about 1,600 BCE in ancient Crete, but the better-known examples are from hundreds of years later in Greece. Crowds thronged to watch Greek boxers fight, and the sport was loved so much by the Romans that they incorporated it into larger events with gladiator games and chariot races.

Boxing as we know it today, though, began in the late 1600s in England. The first set of boxing rules, introduced in 1743, was known as the Broughton's rules. This was the bare-knuckle era, which was later replaced by the London Prize Ring Rules in 1838.

The Marquess of Queensbury Rules, commonly known as the "Queensbury Rules," became the dominant boxing code after 1867 and is still followed, more or less, by all the major boxing promotions. Bare knuckles fighting was eliminated in most promotions by the 1890s.

Despite these rule changes throughout the years, boxing remains pretty much the same sport that was practiced in ancient Greece.

Random Facts:

- There are several boxing organizations throughout the world, but the International Boxing Hall of Fame (IBHF) recognizes four main ones: the International Boxing Federation (IBF), the World Boxing Association (WBA), the World Boxing Council (WBC), and the World Boxing Organization (WBO).
- Muhammad Ali (1942-2016) was born Cassius Marcellus Clay in Louisville, Kentucky. He won a gold medal in the 1960 Summer Olympics and compiling a 56-5 record with 37 knockouts as a professional. He held all of the major titles and won 14 unified title bouts.
- The first title "belt" was presented in 1810 by King George III to Englishman Tom Cribb for defeating former African-American slave Tom Molineaux.
- The Queensbury rules established the standard ring size, the three-minute duration of rounds, the minute between rounds, and the "ten count" among other rules.
- A knockout is when a fighter can't get to their feet after being put on the ground. A "technical knockout" (TKO) is when the referee determines that a fighter has been beaten too much and therefore calls the match.
- A rhyton (drinking vessel) from Crete dated to about 1,550 BCE, known as the "Boxer Rhyton," depicts men boxing and engaging in other combat sports.
- Weight classes weren't introduced until well into the late 1800s and not standardized until the 1900s. There are eight traditional weight class divisions.
- According to Queensbury rules, if a fighter is knocked down three times in a round the referee calls it a TKO.

- The Broughton Rules were the idea of English boxer and boxing promoter Jack Broughton (1703-1789). It included seven rules, many of which later became the basis of the London Prize and Queensbury rules, such as not hitting a boxer who is on the ground.
- The highest-grossing boxing match of all-time was the August 26, 2017 match between undefeated middleweight champion Floyd Mayweather Junior and mixed martial arts champion, Connor McGregor. More than four million people tuned in on pay-per-view to watch Mayweather TKO McGregor in the tenth round. Mayweather earned more than $275 million and McGregor pulled in more than $130 million in the losing effort.
- The evidence indicates that Minoan and Roman boxers wore some clothing, but Greek boxers competed in the nude.
- An "undisputed" champion is a boxer who holds all four of the major title belts.
- Philippines national Manny Pacquiao has won the most championships in the greatest number of weight classes. He has held belts in the flyweight, featherweight, lightweight, and welterweight divisions.
- Although the London Prize Ring Rules allowed for bare knuckles and most boxing matches at that time were still bare knuckles, it added 22 rules to the existing seven Broughton Rules. More rules were added that dealt with how the purses were distributed and the roles of boxers' corner people.
- "Throwing in the towel" is a term used to refer to when a boxer's manager stops the fight because the boxer is getting severely beaten. In the 1800s, throwing a sponge into the ring was a more common sign of submission.
- The style varieties are part of the science behind boxing. "Brawlers" tend to use raw punching power to overcome their

opponent, "counter punchers" are defensive fighters, "out-fighters" use speed and footwork, and "in-fighters" like to get in close and overwhelm their opponents with body blows.

- Mike Tyson was as much a 1980s cultural phenomenon as he was a great boxer. He was the undisputed heavyweight champion from 1987 until 1990 when he lost in a major upset to Buster Douglas. Tyson is the youngest boxer to have won a major title (20).
- An undisputed champion is sometimes considered the "lineal" champion, but more so a lineal champion is either the boxer who defends the undisputed titles against the top challenger or the boxer who defeats the undisputed champion for all the titles. Current undisputed heavyweight champion Tyson Fury is also considered the lineal titleholder.
- Although women's boxing became popular in the 1990s, it has been around since the late 1800s. Catherine "Cat" Davis is one of the first notable American woman boxers, compiling a 12-0 record from 1976-1981.
- The Golden Gloves is an American amateur boxing tournament and organization that began in Chicago in 1927. Muhammad Ali and Joe Louis began their boxing careers in the Golden Gloves organization.

DUELING HISTORY

Western European history is bound up with plenty of honor and a fair amount of egos. The combination of those two occasionally resulted in violence over the centuries in the form of "duels."

Duels came from the European honor code system that held all perceived slights must be dealt with, violently if need be. One of the earliest and best-known examples of single combat comes from Homer's *Iliad*, where the Mycenean hero Achilles fought and killed the Trojan hero Hector.

From mutual combat, duels became more standardized and somewhat ritualized in the 1500s and 1600s. An offense would lead to the offended calling for "satisfaction," which was done through a slap, a dropped glove, or a combination of the two. The "seconds" would then meet to determine the rules of the duel, namely the weapons, the time, and the place where the duel would take place. In the case of a pistol duel, the number of shots was also determined ahead of time.

Early duels were done with swords, but by the 1700s pistols were all the rage. The most famous duel of all was the July 11, 1804 pistol duel between sitting Vice President Aaron Burr and former Secretary of Treasury Alexander Hamilton in New Jersey. Hamilton was shot once in the stomach and died later.

Dueling was illegal in most places when Hamilton met his maker, but a form of dueling continued in the Western states of America until the early 1900s. Gunfights in small Western towns were commonly fought for the same reasons of honor, and just as dueling eventually ended due to laws enacted, the gunfights of the Wild West came to an end when the region was civilized.

Random Facts:

- Although dueling was technically illegal in New Jersey, Hamilton and Burr decided to fight their duel there because the authorities usually didn't prosecute duelers.
- A Polish honor code was written in 1919 by Wladyslaw Boziewicz that details the reasons that can lead to a duel and how to carry out a proper duel in Poland, although dueling had long been illegal there by that time.
- Although women have fought duels against other women in history, it's extremely rare. More often, duels were fought by men over women's sexual honor/reputation.
- The Russian dueling code forbade men of different ranks from dueling each other.
- California United States Senator David C. Broderick and former Chief Justice of the California Supreme Court, David S. Terry, fought a duel on September 13, 1859, in San Francisco, California. Broderick was killed and Terry was arrested, but the case was dismissed. It's considered the last true duel in American history.
- Hamilton's oldest son, Philip Hamilton (1782-1801), was killed in a duel in Weehauken, New Jersey, which was also where Alexander later met his fate.
- Most pistol duels ended without bloodshed. The seconds often convinced the primaries to fire their guns in the air, which ended the duel and the offended received his satisfaction.
- Europeans brought the dueling tradition to the Americas in the 1600s, where it gained popularity in the 1700s and 1800s. Dueling with knives known as *facones* was common in Argentina in the 1800s.
- Hamilton and Burr used Wogdon & Barton flintlock pistols in their duel.

- Viking duels were called *holmgang*. They usually consisted of the two men fighting it out on a small island.
- The Hamilton-Burr duel was the result of long-simmering personal conflicts between the two men. Hamilton was known to be acerbic and often criticized Burr publicly, to the point of slander. Burr was the one to issue the challenge.
- Dueling was decriminalized in Uruguay in 1920 and not outlawed again until 1992.
- The first written dueling codes were written in Italy during the Renaissance and were known as *code duello*.
- Another famous Wild West gunfight/duel took place on April 5, 1879, at the famous Long Branch Saloon in Dodge City, Kansas between 19-year-old Frank Loving and 48-year-old Levi Richardson. Richardson bullied Loving into a fight, but Loving killed the bully. He was never charged with a crime as the authorities ruled it self-defense.
- The rapier was the weapon of choice in most sword duels.
- Dueling was popular in Japan among the samurai in the 1500s and 1600s. Miyamoto Musashi (1584-1645) the author of *The Book of the Five Rings*, is said to have won 60 duels.
- Most pistol duels involved each dueler having one shot each, with the duelers taking turns to fire their shots. Three shots were usually the maximum allowed.
- The challenger usually decided on the type of weapon used in a duel, although that was not necessarily always the case.
- Two British Prime Ministers—William Pitt the Younger and the Duke of Wellington—fought duels while in office.
- After the Hamilton-Burr duel, Burr was charged with murder in New Jersey, but the charges were dropped. He hid out in Georgia for a time, though he returned to the White

NATIONAL PARKS

The idea of conserving wilderness lands started to become popular in the early 1800s when it became apparent that progress was moving pretty quickly; too quickly, in some areas. American President Andrew Jackson signed legislation in 1832 that protected land near what is now Hot Springs, Arkansas and, in 1864, President Lincoln signed a bill into law that prohibited what is now Yosemite National Park from being settled.

These early efforts were followed up by the lifelong campaign of American conservationist John Muir (1838-1914). Muir played a big role in the conservation of Yosemite and is therefore often thought of as the father of national parks. However, that honor truly belongs to a geologist named Ferdinand Hayden.

Hayden explored the region around Yellowstone in 1871, which was primarily located in Wyoming Territory. It was a rough and tough time and place in American history, especially in the West: the Sioux tribes were supreme on the Great Plains and Custer was still five years from meeting his last stand. Most Americans had little interest in the Western territories and any interest they did have was primarily centered on newly-discovered gold and silver deposits.

Future President Theodore Roosevelt gave his support to the project and in 1872 Congress made Yellowstone the United States'—and the world's—first national park.

Today, national parks are on every continent except Antarctica and are as diverse in their size, type, and facilities as the countries in which they are located. Many, if not most, national parks are known for their natural beauty, while for some, such as Kruger National, the wildlife is the primary attraction.

Random Facts:

- Australia has more national parks than any other nation at 685. Far behind in second place, but with a still very respectable 147 parks, is Thailand.
- Kruger National Park was established in 1926 as South Africa's first national park. It is one of South Africa's primary tourist destinations, drawing about 1.5 million per year.
- Each nation that has national parks administers them through a government agency. In the United States, the U.S. National Parks Service oversees all the parks.
- Brazil has the most national parks in South America with 72, but Argentina has the distinction of having the oldest national park on the continent. Chile is the South American country with the most land being dedicated to national parks, at just over 19%.
- The Uluṟu-Kata Tjuṯa National Park in Northern Territory, Australia is named for Uluru (formerly Ayers Rock) and a similar large rock formation located 25 miles away, Tjuṯa.
- Northeast Greenland National Park, Greenland is the largest national park in the world. It was established in 1974 and covers nearly 375,000 square miles. It covers nearly half the country and since Greenland is such a large country, it is also larger than all but 29 countries.
- Mexico has the most national parks in North America with 67. The United States is second with 62.
- At only 39 square miles in area, Göreme National Park in Turkey is not one of the bigger national parks, but it is certainly one of the most fascinating. The park is known for its elaborate underground dwellings and monasteries that were built from the 400s to through the 800s CE.

- The Great Smoky Mountains National Park in Tennessee and North Carolina, USA is the most visited national park in the world. It attracts about nine million visitors per year.
- If you don't mind spending your vacation with crab-eating macaques, then you may want to visit Penang National Park in Malaysia. Known for its pristine beaches, one of those beaches, "Monkey Beach," is populated by macaques, which are for the most part harmless, although they are known to swipe bags and articles off unsuspecting tourists.
- Although many people believe that Penang is the smallest national park in the world, that honor goes to Le Parc National des Iles de la Madeleine, Senegal. It is just a tiny 0.17 square mile island off the coast of Dakar.
- More than 25% of Costa Rica's land area is inside its 29 national parks. Costa Rica's national parks have become a popular "eco-tourism" destination since the 1990s.
- Canada's national parks cover more than 230,000 square miles, while the U.S.'s encompasses more than 130,000 square miles and Mexico's covers nearly 9,000 square miles.
- If you want to view endangered Bengal tigers in their natural habitat, Ranthambore National Park, India, is the place to go. The 515 square mile park was established in 1980 to preserve the animal that symbolizes the country and to give visitors and chance to see the majestic beasts in the wild.
- The Grand Prismatic Spring in Yellowstone Park is the third-largest in the world but is more known for its bright colors, which are the result of microbes that live in the spring.
- Yosemite National Park, California was the sight of a phenomenal UFO sighting on September 19, 2002. A large number of park visitors captured the strange lights on film but no explanation has been given and UFO sightings continue over the park.

- Besides UFO sightings, national parks can be creepy, with people sometimes disappearing, never to be found. In 1996, a German family disappeared from Death Valley National Park, California without a trace. Authorities believe that skeletal remains discovered in 2009 are those of the missing family.
- Plitvice Lakes National Park in Croatia is one of the most popular national parks in Europe. More than one million visitors travel to Plitvice every year to gaze at its wonderful waterfalls and cascade lakes.
- If you're a winter person, then Banff National Park in Alberta, Canada is your place. Located high in the Canadian Rocky Mountains, more than three million visitors come to Banff every year to see grizzly bears and mountain lions and to ski during the winter.
- Royal National Park in New South Wales, Australia, is the second-oldest national park in the world. It was established in 1879.

SATURDAY MORNING CARTOONS

If you're an American born between the early 1960s and the late 1980s, then you probably have fond memories of Saturday mornings. You probably remember how you and your siblings would get up before your parents, race downstairs to the family television set, and put on your favorite cartoons. I personally liked *Captain Caveman, Hong Kong Phooey*, and *Scooby-Doo*, but there were tons to choose from.

The trend began in the 1960s when executives from the big three networks—ABC, CBS, and NBC—saw an untapped goldmine of potential. On Saturday mornings, kids were home from school and their parents were often home from work, but they were usually busy doing chores. So, the idea of creating relatively cheap animated programing for this timeslot was pitched by animation companies.

The networks loved the idea and especially loved the advertising money revenue that came flowing from toy companies and other children-themed products.

The format was an instant ratings and advertising success, but some parent groups had a problem with what they thought was a lack of educational content. There was also a big push to eliminate violence on television at the time, so to keep the angry parents at bay, the networks began airing interstitial programming during the 1970s.

The most popular and famous of these was the series *Schoolhouse Rock!* on ABC, but each network had similar educational-themed interstitial programming.

By the late 1980s, American culture had changed and the Saturday morning cartoons would become the victim. A combination of the growth of cable television and VCRs meant that kids had other options. So, by the late 1990s, the phenomenon of Saturday morning cartoons was all but over.

Random Facts:

- Another nail in the coffin of Saturday morning cartoons was the introduction of weekday first-run syndication cartoons. Shows like *G.I. Joe, The Transformers, He-Man and the Masters of the Universe,* and *She-Ra: Princess of Power* offered kids a daily fill of animated fun.
- Hanna-Barbera Productions was the animation company that started the Saturday morning cartoon craze. Founded in 1957 by artists and animators William Hanna and Joseph Barbera, they produced some of the most memorable early Saturday morning cartoons, including *Tom and Jerry, Space Ghost,* and *Scooby-Doo.*
- There were several trends during the lifespan of Saturday morning cartoons that changed the content matter and style of the shows. For instance, many popular live-action television shows were animated during the 1970s, including *Star Trek: The Animated Series* and *The New Adventures of Gilligan.*
- The late Casey Kasem (1932-2014) is best known for being the host of the American radio show *American Top 40,* but he was also an accomplished voice actor. Kasem's most notable Saturday morning role was as the voice of Shaggy from *Scooby-Do.* He also voiced superhero Robin for *Superfriends* and Alexander Cabot III on *Josie and the Pussycats.*
- Perhaps one of the most forgettable Saturday morning cartoons was *Hammerman,* which ran on ABC in 1991. It was about a social worker who doubled as a superhero, voiced by none other than rapper MC Hammer.
- Scooby-Doo is probably the most recognizable and popular Saturday morning cartoon character. After the success of the original show *Scooby-Do, Where Are You?* in 1969, Scooby Doo has appeared in dozens of other sequel series, related shows, and movies.

- Filmation Associates challenged Hanna-Barbera as the biggest animation company from 1963 to 1989. Filmation created plenty of Saturday morning cartoons that were more action orientation, including *Flash Gordon* and *Tarzan, Lord of the Jungle*.
- Although both *The Flintstones* and *The Jetsons* were Hanna-Barbera animated series, they were prime-time shows. After its initial run in prime-time, though, *The Jetsons* was shown on Saturday mornings in some markets.
- If you watched enough Saturday morning cartoons, then you probably recognize the name Iwao Takamoto (1925-2007). He began his career as an illustrator and worked his way up to produce many of Hanna-Barbara's biggest hits in the 1970s.
- Most Saturday morning cartoons had limited episodes, with 20 episodes being standard even for hit shows.
- The voice of the character Space Ghost as well as Blue Falcon of *Dynomutt, Dog Wonder* was done by Gary Owens (1934-2015). Owens was also the announcer on the popular sketch comedy show *Rowan and Martin's Laugh-In*.
- Rotoscoping was an animation technique that was commonly used by Filmation. The technique involves tracing images over several frames to create the effect of movement.
- *Schoolhouse Rock!* first aired in 1973 and ran until 1985. It was brought back briefly in the 1990s and 2000s, but it wasn't nearly as popular or influential as it was in the '70s and '80s.
- The improvement in and lowered cost of home video game systems have also been cited as another reason for the demise of Saturday morning cartoons.
- Artist Walter Lantz created the iconic Woody Woodpecker cartoon character in 1940, more than 20 years before the rise of Saturday morning cartoons. It would be nearly 60 years before Woody made it to Saturday mornings when *The New Woody Woodpecker Show* ran on Fox from 1999 to 2002.

- If you ever had the chance to see *The New Fantastic Four* series, which NBC ran on Saturday mornings in 1978, you may be wondering what happened to the Human Torch in more recent versions. The notable flame-throwing superhero was replaced by a robot named H.E.R.B.I.E., but contrary to urban myth, it wasn't because the network was afraid of lawsuits if kids started fires trying to be the Human Torch. No, the Torch's absence was because Universal Studios did not release the rights to the character.
- Running from 1965 to 1969 on ABC, the cartoon *The Beatles* followed the members of the famous rock band on many adventures. Curiously, the band members were voiced by actors!
- Hal Sutherland (1929-2014) was one of Filmation's primary artists, so if you're familiar with Saturday morning cartoons, you've no doubt seen his name in credits.
- Long before his fall from grace, actor and comedian Bill Cosby was a fixture every Saturday morning in America when his *Fat Albert and the Cosby Kids* ran for 13 years on CBS and first-run syndication. Filmation did the animation, but Cosby wrote the scripts and did many of the voices.
- What do you get when you mix Hanna-Barbara, the Jetsons, and a popular 1970s musically talented family? *Partridge Family 2200 A.D.* featured the famous TV family navigating life in the future. Needless to say, it wasn't a hit with the kids and only lasted 16 episodes.

WILL THE REAL SHAKESPEARE PLEASE STAND UP?

English playwright and author William Shakespeare (1564-1616) is rightly considered one of the greatest literary artists to have used the English language. He has been credited with 39 plays, including *A Midsummer's Night Dream* and *Julius Caesar,* and more than 154 sonnets. Although Shakespeare died at the relatively young age of 51, his flame burned bright and his legacy can be found in nearly every library, bookstore, and schools of all levels.

Chances are you've read a Shakespeare play or two while in high school and/or college.

The writings of Shakespeare have influenced generations of later writers and his style has been emulated by countless more hoping to break into the business.

There's no doubt that, as far as writers go, Shakespeare had a profound influence on literature—and history, for that matter. But there's also no doubt that Shakespeare was somewhat of an enigmatic person. Questions about what Shakespeare looked like, the religion he practiced, and even the authorship of his works have circulated.

Some have postulated that since no written description of Shakespeare is known to exist, that he was a fictional character. Those who believe this idea, or variations of it, assert that one or more other people wrote Shakespeare's classics. There have been nearly 100 claims to authorship of Shakespeare's works by people other than Shakespeare, but the most popular is the so-called "Oxfordian theory."

According to the Oxfordian theory, Edward de Vere, the 17th Earl of Oxford, was the true author of Shakespeare's works. Those who believe in the Oxford theory argue that Shakespeare's plays and poems were autobiographical and more closely fit the life of de Vere than they do Shakespeare's.

The Oxford theory, and the other alternate author theories of Shakespeare's works, became popular in the 1800s, but they have for the most part been ruled out by historians and literary experts.

Random Facts:

- Francis Bacon (1561-1626) was a well-known British philosopher who some believed was Shakespeare. The theory is based on philosophical ideas first proposed by Bacon that are also prevalent in Shakespeare's works.
- Because Shakespeare was born at Stratford-upon-Avon, those who propose alternative authorship theories of his works are called "Anti-Stratfordians."
- The first alternative theory of Shakespeare's authorship was the "Bacon" theory, which was later followed by the Oxford theory.
- One theory that has come up from time to time is that Oxford was part of a collective that wrote the works together.
- Another alternate theory that was popular for a while has British playwright Christopher Marlow (1564-1593) as the true author of Shakespeare's works. The theory goes that Marlow faked his death and continued to write as Shakespeare.
- The general Anti-Stratfordian argument contends that Shakespeare's works demonstrate a broad knowledge of history, languages, and cultures that someone with his humble, middle-class background simply wouldn't have had.
- The name "Shakespeare" was spelled differently on the titles of his works and was signed with different spellings by him throughout his life. Some of the spellings included: William Shaksper, William Shakspere, and William Shakspeare.
- Most of the alternate theories of Shakespeare's authorship arose in the late 1800s and declined by the mid-1900s.
- The Shakespeare Fellowship was an organization that formed in 1921 to promote Anti-Stratfordian theories, but it eventually became a pro-Oxford group. In 2013, it merged with another pro-

Oxford group, the Shakespeare Oxford Society, to form the Shakespeare Oxford Fellowship.

- One of the major blows against the Anti-Stratfordian theories is that Shakespeare was recognized in the writings and statements of other writers and actors from his time. There's no reason to believe they would have recognized him if "Shakespeare" was only a pen name.
- It's believed that the first documented reference that questioned Shakespeare's identity was in the 1848 book *The Romance of Yachting* by American author Joseph C. Hart.
- Many mid-20th century French writers believed that William Stanley, 6th Earl of Derby (1561-1642) was the true author of Shakespeare's works. This became known as the Derbyite theory.
- A more recent and less popular theory is that Sir Henry Neville (1564-1615) was Shakespeare. The Nevellian theory, as it's known, was first proposed in 2005.
- Nearly all of the Anti-Stratfordian theories believe that English playwright Ben Johnson (1572-1637) was the source of the conspiracy to cover the true identity of the person who supposedly wrote Shakespeare's works. Although Johnson and Shakespeare were contemporaries and by many accounts friends, none of the theories explain why Johnson, who was quite successful in his own right, would go to such elaborate lengths to steal others' works on behalf of Shakespeare.
- A 1963 episode of the American television show *The Twilight Zone* approaches the Anti-Stratfordian theories from the opposite angle. In the episode, a struggling writer finds a book of black magic that he uses to summon Shakespeare, who then helps his television writing career. The TV writer, though, refuses to give Shakespeare credit.
- Another Anti-Stratfordian theory that links Bacon to Shakespeare

states that the writings were part of an elaborate conspiracy by the secret society of Rosicrucian's.

- Even former Libyan dictator Muammar Gaddafi (1942-2011) got into the Anti-Stratfordian scene when he publicly supported the theory that Zubayr bin William, a somewhat obscure Arab scholar, was the author of Shakespeare's writings.
- It's not just men who have been attributed as the true Shakespeare. Some believe that Shakespeare's wife, Anne Hathaway (1556-1623), was the true brains behind the masterpieces, while others think it was a previous girlfriend named Anne Whateley.
- Although most academics are opposed to Anti-Stratfordian theories, some notable people have supported the Oxford theory. United States Supreme Court Justice Anton Scalia, actor Jeremy Irons, and Sigmund Freud were all believers in Oxfordism.
- Believers in the Bacon theory argue that Shakespeare's writing is full of secret codes, or "ciphers," that relate the true identity of the writer.

THE NEW WONDERS OF THE WORLD

We began this chapter by looking at the Seven Wonders of the Ancient World, so we'll end it by examining what many consider just as amazing wonders. The original list has been inspiring to historians, artists, and architects throughout history, but it's limited.

The fact that only one of the original wonders still stands doesn't help. So, in more recent decades, there have been calls for new lists to include "modern wonders" and others have called for a new list of modern and pre-modern wonders.

In 2000, a campaign was started by a man named Bernard Weber (Canadian-Swiss) to pick seven new wonders. Weber took advantage of the burgeoning Internet Age by making voting available to anyone in the world online and named the new campaign "the New7Wonders of the World."

After eliminating hundreds of entries, the final New7Wonders were announced in 2007 as the following: the Great Wall of China, China; Petra, Jordan; the Colosseum in Rome, Italy; Chichen Itza, Mexico; Machu Picchu, Peru; Taj Mahal, India; the Christ the Redeemer statue, Brazil. Since it is so awesome and is the only remaining monument from the original list, the Khufu's Pyramid in Giza, Egypt was also included as an honorary member.

Some impressive wonders just missed the cut for the New7Wonders, so other people began compiling alternate lists of modern wonders.

The American Society of Civil Engineers picked their own Seven Wonders of the Modern World, which is very engineering and scientifically based yet no less impressive. The list includes the following: the Channel Tunnel/Chunnel, United Kingdom-France; the CN Tower, Canada; the Empire State Building, United States; the Golden Gate Bridge, United States; the Itaipu Dam, Brazil-Paraguay; the Netherlands Protective Sea Wall, Netherlands; and the Panama Canal, Panama.

I'm sure if you think about it long enough, you can come up with a list of your own!

Random Facts:

- The dating of the Great Wall is open to debate since some of it can be traced back to the 5th Dynasty BCE, but it wasn't completed until the Ming Dynasty (1368-1644)
- The CN Tower is located in Toronto, Ontario. The tower stands 1,815 feet, which was enough to make it the tallest freestanding structure in the world for 32 years. Today, it's third in that category.
- The city of Petra was built in a valley in Jordan by an ethnic group known as the Nabateans in the 5th century BCE. It served as a way station along the trade routes between the Levant and Mesopotamia.
- Russia has no site listed on any of the wonders of the world lists, but Red Square in Moscow was a finalist for the New7Wonders. Red Square is the location of the historic St. Basil's Cathedral, which was consecrated by Macarius Metropolitan of Moscow in 1561.
- Tourist and commerce ministries in various countries led voting campaigns to have monuments in their countries added to the New7Wonders list.
- Nearly one-third of the Netherlands is below sea level and two-thirds of the country is susceptible to flooding, which led to the creation of the seawall in phases. A system of dams known as the Zuiderzee works reclaimed land from the sea because of the vast flooding that would occur. This work created a freshwater lake in 1932-1933. After flooding in 1953, the Delta Works were initiated to claim more land and support existing dikes and dams.
- There are no wonders from Australia on the New7Wonders list.
- The Cable News Network compiled a list of the Seven Natural Wonders of the World, which included the following: Victoria

Falls, Zambia and Zimbabwe; Paricutin volcano, Mexico; Mount Everest, Nepal; Great Barrier Reef, Australia: Aurora Borealis and Aurora Australis, Arctic and Antarctic; Grand Canyon, United States; Rio de Janeiro Harbor, Brazil.

- Work on the Panama Canal began in 1881 and wasn't finished until 1914. Officially, 5,609 workers died building the canal. An estimated 12,000 workers had died during the construction of the Panama Railway and over 22,000 during the French effort to build a canal. Many of these deaths were due to disease, particularly yellow fever and malaria.
- The Colosseum of Rome is the only New7Wonders located in Europe.
- Construction on the Taj Mahal began in 1632 and it wasn't completed until 1653. It was the idea of the Mughal Emperor Shah Jahan to serve as a tomb for his favorite wife. The emperor lived to see the completion of the monument and was buried there next to his wife in 1658.
- The Internet was chosen as one of the "New Seven Wonders," not to be confused with the New7Wonders, by a group of judges as part of a promotion by the American newspaper *USA Today* and the television show *Good Morning America.*
- The Itaipu Dam provides power to 90% of Paraguay. Construction on the dam began in 1971 and was completed in 1982, as a joint partnership between the Brazilian and Paraguayan governments.
- Many people were surprised when the Leaning Tower of Pisa wasn't even a finalist for the New7Wonders of the World. Due to a combination of its architecture and its obvious tilt, the Leaning Tower has been included on many unofficial lists of world wonders since the original Seven Wonders of the World list.
- The iconic Sydney Opera House was a finalist for the New7Wonders, but it wasn't included in the Seven Wonders of the Modern World.

- The Empire State Building seems somewhat quaint today compared to some of the behemoth skyscrapers that have been built in the Middle East in recent years, but its construction was an incredible feat for the time. It took just over a year to construct the building (March 1930 to April 1931) and it was the first building to have more than 100 floors. It was the tallest building in the world until 1970.
- The city of Timbuktu, Mali was one of the finalists to narrowly miss out on being included on the New7Wonders list. Besides its great sounding name, Timbuktu is known for the unique architecture of its mosques and other holy sites that date to the 16th century.
- Chichen Itza was a major Maya city from 600-900 CE. The centerpiece of the city is the pyramid of Kukulkan.
- The Christ the Redeemer statue was the idea of local Brazilian Catholic groups. The primary engineer was Brazilian Heitor da Silva Costa and the main sculptor was Frenchman Paul Landowski.
- The Moais (giant stone heads) of Easter Island finished eighth in the voting for the New7Wonders of the world.
- It took ten years to complete the Colosseum (72-82 CE). It was begun during the reign of the Emperor Vespasian and completed during Titus' rule.

HAPPY DAYS ARE HERE AGAIN

Few people will argue that the invention of the television had a monumental impact on modern society. It changed the way we receive our news and it became the leading form of entertainment for millions of people around the world. Even after the invention of the Internet and the lowering in prices of home computers, TV continues to hold strong in the world of home electronics.

You'll find a TV set in nearly every home in the most industrialized countries and televisions are even now widely available in many developing countries. Many homes may have more than one TV.

So, how did television become such a ubiquitous part of everyday life for most people?

You may be surprised to know that the invention of the television wasn't an "ah-ha" moment but was the result of a long process that began in the 1800s. After several versions of image projecting devices were invented, television as we know it—electronic television that uses cathode rays—was invented in 1897. It took some time to make television available to consumers, but by the 1930s, companies were selling the earliest TV sets.

But there was one problem: there was nothing to watch!

Well, that isn't entirely true. There were some shows produced in the 1930s using what is known as the "mechanical television process", but once electronic television became the norm in the 1940s, everything changed, ushering in the first Golden Age of Television.

Although most networks in the 1940s and '50s only broadcast for a few hours a day and the programming was limited, ratings were immediately huge for television of any kind. Variety shows and anthologies were popular early and by the 1950s, comedies such as *I Love Lucy* and *The Honeymooners* and Westerns like *Gunsmoke* were the most common genres on TV. This initial explosion in the use and popularity of television set the tone that has lasted until the present.

Random Facts:

- The *Kraft Television Theatre* was an early, successful television show. It was an anthology drama that aired from 1947 to 1958.
- Many television programs and events from the 1940s became what are known as "lost television broadcasts." These are television shows of which all archives have been lost. Most of the seasons from the sitcom *The Goldbergs* (1949-1956)—yes, there was an original Goldbergs!—were lost.
- Many TV shows in the 1940s were broadcast in a 15-minute format.
- The first live sports event to be broadcast on television in the United States was a May 17, 1939 baseball game between the Columbia Lions and the Princeton Tigers.
- Lots of television shows from the 1940s and '50s began as radio programs and continued to run concurrently as such once the medium of television became more popular. *Gunsmoke (1955-75)* is one of the more notable television shows to have begun on radio and ran concurrently on television for several years.
- Television sets cost between: $129 to $1,295 in the 1950s. A basic 17-inch black-and-white was the cheapest, but if you wanted to impress everyone on your block, you could dole out at least $1,000 for a color set. The only problem was that most shows made in the 1950s were still done in black and white!
- During the 1940s and '50s NBC, ABC, CBS, and Fox weren't the four major television networks; instead, it was NBC, ABC, CBS, and Dumont. The Dumont Television network (1946-56) was ahead of the TV curve in many ways. After numerous problems, Dumont ceased operations in 1956 and as a result, many of its shows became "lost television broadcasts."

- Although the popular sitcom *Happy Days* ran in the 1970s and '80s, it was about American life in the 1950s. The show regularly featured the Cunningham family gathered around a television set watching shows from the era such as *The Jack Benny Show* and *Texaco Star Theatre* starring Milton Berle.
- Many of the most popular shows from the 1940s and '50s were done live in studios. By the late 1950s, videotape was being used to record shows.
- News reports and shows were created along with the earliest TV shows, although they were quite different from what they are today. Early network news broadcasts were usually 15 minutes long and were often supplemented by local news broadcasts. By the 1950s, most networks transitioned to the 30-minute news format.
- Television truly threatened to make the radio obsolete, but the invention and release of the first transistor radio in 1954 saved the device from obscurity.
- The 1950s saw the emergence of many family comedies that are still popular today in reruns. Some of these include *Father Knows Best, Leave it to Beaver,* and *The Donna Reed Show.*
- Unlike today, television studios in the 1940s and '50s were on the East Coast of the United States.
- Most Western countries experienced a golden age of television during the relatively same period as the United States, especially the English-speaking countries.
- In Latin America, TV networks began broadcasting a little later than the U.S., so their golden eras of television began later. Television began broadcasting in Mexico in 1946, in Brazil in 1950, in Argentina in 1951, and in Chile in 1957.
- *Gunsmoke* began as a radio show in 1952 before transitioning to the small screen in 1955. It ran for 20 years with 635 episodes.

Gunsmoke held the record for most scripted shows produced until it was finally beaten by *The Simpsons* in 2018.

- The 1947 World Series between the New York Yankees and the Brooklyn Dodgers was the first to be broadcast on television and was watched by over 3.9 million viewers.
- NBC broadcasted the first National Football League game on October 22, 1939, between the Philadelphia Eagles and the Brooklyn Dodgers. The first live games were broadcast in the 1950s by the Dumont network.
- South Africa didn't begin broadcasting television until 1976. The apartheid government believed that television would be a bad influence on its people.
- Due to changing consumer tastes, few of the shows that were screened in the 1950s made it into the 1960s. Sci-fi anthology series *The Twilight Zone* was one of the few exceptions, lasting until 1964.

BEER AND WINE IN THE ANCIENT WORLD

Earlier, we looked at how alcohol is distilled and some of the drinks that are made from "spirits," so now let's look at the oldest and simplest forms of alcoholic beverages.

Beer and wine were the first types of alcoholic beverages to be made because they don't require much equipment or knowledge. Although the ingredients used to make each are a little different, the processes are pretty much the same. Beer and wine are made through the process of fermentation. Beer is generally made with a variety of different cereals with sugar added while wine is made from fermented grapes and sugar.

Civilization began in ancient Egypt and in ancient Mesopotamia around the same time (3,100 BCE) and although the two cultures are separated by about 1,000 miles, they shared many features, including the earliest production of beer and wine.

An ancient Sumerian poem describes how barley was used in Mesopotamia to make beer and wine is mentioned throughout the Bible.

For the ancient Egyptians, beer was often used as a substitute for water, because the water from the Nile River was not drinkable. On the other hand, wine was the drink of the nobles. Reliefs from the New Kingdom temples in Egypt show nobles drinking wine at ostentatious parties.

They may have lacked technology, but the ancient Egyptians still knew how to have a good time!

Random Facts:

- During the New Kingdom (c. 1,500-1,075 BCE) in ancient Egypt, religious festivals were quite common. Drunkenness was often encouraged at the festivals.
- Resinated wine, known as "retsina," is believed to have originated in ancient Greece and has been made for over 2,000 years.
- The ancient Egyptian word for wine was *irep*.
- If you were to see Mesopotamian or Egyptian beer today, you probably wouldn't recognize it as beer. Mesopotamian beer was so thick and gruel-like that a straw or spoon was needed to drink it.
- The ancient Egyptian word for beer was *henqet*.
- As with wine today, ancient Egyptian wine was primarily made from grapes, but palm and date wine were also popular.
- *Bouza* is a fermented alcoholic drink popular in North Africa and parts of the Middle East. It's believed that it originated in ancient Nubia.
- The Romans knew beer as *cerevisa* in the Latin language. If you're familiar with Spanish, then you can see the origin of the word for beer in that language.
- "Viticulture" is the term for wine growing.
- Although Egypt and Mesopotamia may be home to the world's first civilizations, Armenia is home to the world's first winery. The "Areni-1" winery (over 6,100 years old) is a cave complex where wine was manufactured around 4,100 BCE.
- The earliest evidence of fermented drinks in China dates back to around 7,000 BCE. The ancient Chinese used grapes and rice to make their alcoholic drinks.

- Ancient Egyptian beer had a high nutritional value but with a low alcohol by volume (ABV) percentage, so it was consumed throughout the workday. The men who worked on the pyramids, temples, and tombs of Egypt were paid in beer, among other commodities.
- The ancient Sumerian goddess, Ninkasi, was the patroness of beer. She was obscure by Mesopotamian standards, although she was worshipped by peoples in the region who came after the Sumerians.
- Beer plays a major role in the ancient Egyptian myth *The Destruction of Mankind*. As the lioness goddess, Sekhmet, is destroying humankind and drinking human blood, the sun-god orders that beer mixed with red ochre be given to her to trick her and save humanity.
- The "Law Code of Hammurabi" was written around 1,754 BCE. It's known for the details it relates of a variety of offenses, some of which included who could work in bars and how long they could be kept open.
- Offering valuable to the gods and goddesses was important in ancient cultures. In ancient Egypt, the *Hetep Di Nisu* or "royal offering" formula usually included gifts of wine *and* beer. An Egyptian doctor named Udjahorresnet, who lived in the 6th century BCE, even offered the god Osiris, 1,000 beers!
- The Sumerians introduced the process of using *bappir*, a twice-baked barley bread, in the brewing process. Later peoples in Mesopotamia also used the process.
- The long history of Italian wine began with the Romans. The Romans learned many of their wine-making ideas from the Greeks, but by the 2nd century BCE, large vineyards were common in Italy.
- The 1st century BCE Greek historian, Diodorus, traveled through

Egypt and noted that they produced a barley drink called *zythos,* "the bouquet of which is not much inferior to that of wine."

- Wine may have been the drink of nobles in Egypt, but all classes of Romans, even slaves, consumed wine daily, even as they worked.

PURPLE ROBES, SCEPTERS, AND CROOKS AND FLAILS

The days of absolute monarchies are long past, but there are still a couple left in the world and there are also still some constitutional monarchies. The majority of us view these royals as a bit of anachronism, especially with all their royal accouterments and regalia, which seem like ancient relics more than anything. The reality is that, for the most part, they *are* relics from another era.

Kings and queens have been setting themselves apart from their subjects through their attire pretty much since the dawn of civilization 5,000 years ago. The kings of Mesopotamia weren't too ostentatious, distinguishing themselves with simple oval crowns and large beards, but their contemporaries in Egypt truly wanted everyone to know they were kings.

Egyptian royal regalia included the crook, flail, and false beard and of course a crown. The standard Egyptian crown was known as the "double crown" because it was two crowns that separated the two distinct regions of Egypt: Upper and Lower Egypt. The Egyptian kings also had several other crowns for a variety of different occasions.

The Persians adopted the Mesopotamian royal beard style but also introduced more elaborate crowns and purple robes in the 6th century BCE. Purple became the color of royalty because the dye that made it was so rare.

By the time of the Middle Age in Europe, royal regalia became much more elaborate and ritualized, although it was still the fashion statement it was for the Egyptians.

Random Facts:

- The *globus cruciger* became a popular form of regalia for European kings in the Middle Ages. It's a cross on top of an orb and represents Christ's dominion over the world.
- In ancient Egypt, the crown of Lower Egypt was red and the crown of Upper Egypt was white. The white crown would be technically placed inside the red crown, although in pictorial art, they appear as one crown.
- The *palin* is the type of throne the ruling monarch of Burma sits upon.
- The "Crown Jewels of the United Kingdom" includes all the royal regalia used at coronations. They are housed in the Tower of London and include some of the following: a *globus cruciger*, scepters, and the crown.
- The mace is a traditional symbol of royal authority that can be traced back more than 5,000 years. The king using the mace to destroy Egypt's enemies was a common artistic motif from 3,100 BCE onward.
- The *triregnum* or papal tiara was the crown worn by each pope until 1963.
- The purple dye in royal robes was known as "Tyrian purple." It is a secretion produced by several species of predatory sea snails in the family Muricidae, rock snails originally known by the name 'Murex'. In ancient times, extracting this dye involved tens of thousands of snails and substantial labor, and as a result, the dye was highly valued.
- The long, thin beard worn by ancient Egyptian was held in place by a strap that goes around the head. If you look closely at statues of Egyptian kings, you can usually see the strap.

- The Thai monarchy employs regalia that comes from native, Buddhist, and Hindu traditions. Several weapons play an important role in coronations, including the "Sword of Victory."
- Although early Muslim caliphs were fairly austere in their dress, the Ottoman sultans were somewhat extravagant with their dress and regalia. The sultans wore many different crowns.
- Japanese imperial regalia once included the "Three Sacred Treasures": the sword "Kusanagi no Tsurugi," the mirror "Yata no Kagami," and the jewel "Yasakani no Magatama." The sword no longer exists.
- The Romans were not big on royalty or regalia, but a laurel wreath crown was awarded for military victories.
- The meaning of the crook and flail in Egyptian kingship is a matter of debate, but it may represent the pharaoh as a shepherd of his people (crook), who occasionally has to use force (flail).
- Although Nigeria is a democratic country with no monarchy, it's also a federal republic with several different tribal groups. Some of the tribes from different regions have kept their ceremonial titles and regalia.
- The "Dragon Throne" was the name of the throne in imperial China. Like the modern term "White House," Dragon Throne could refer to the physical throne the emperor sat on, or the emperor himself.
- The regalia of the defunct Holy Roman Empire is housed in the Imperial Treasury of the Hofburg palace in Vienna, Austria.
- The rod that modern popes carry in public and for ceremonies is known as the "papal ferula."
- After Napoleon proclaimed himself emperor, he had a new set of imperial regalia made, which included a crown and throne for his December 2, 1804 coronation.

- Although the Bolsheviks murdered the Russian royal family in 1918, they kept the Russian crown jewels/regalia in storage. The regalia is now on public view at the Kremlin Armoury Museum.
- Other crowns worn by Egyptian kings included the *atef* crown, the blue crown, and the *hemhem* crown.

THESE FANS TAKE THEIR SPORTS TOO SERIOUSLY

We've chronicled in this book how fans around the world love a variety of different sports and share that love across national borders. But unfortunately, some fans take that love a little too far and turn it into a violent obsession.

I'm talking about the phenomenon of sports hooliganism.

"Hooliganism," of course, refers to violence by obsessive sports fans, usually in or around the stadium but not necessarily. The origins of the word hooliganism are a bit murky, although it is believed to have come from England in the late 1800s. England is also the country best known for the hooliganism of its association football fans.

Hooliganism was sporadic and unorganized until after World War II when supporters of teams began organizing into what are known as "firms." The firms challenged each other inside and outside the stadiums. By the 1960s, firms were popping up all over Europe.

Although law enforcement has heavily cracked down on British firms in recent years, football hooliganism has grown in Eastern Europe.

But Europe is not the only place where hooliganism is a problem and association football is not the only place where it happens. In addition to association football, hooliganism and sports violence, organized and unorganized, has been associated with hockey, basketball, and different codes of football and has taken place on every continent.

Random Facts:

- Although fan violence is less organized in North America, it's far from absent. Most fan violence in North America has taken place in cities where a team has won a major championship.
- One of the most heated on-the-field rivalries in the English Premier League, between West Ham United and Millwall, is also the most violent firm rivalry. West Ham United's firm is known as the "Inter City Firm," while the Millwall firm is called the "Bushwackers."
- During communism, many of the sports clubs in the Eastern Bloc were multi-sports endeavors, including association football, basketball, hockey, and other sports. Many of those clubs are still organized that way today, so their supporters, and hooligan firms, can be found fighting at a variety of different sporting events.
- The worst sports fan violence in African history took place on May 9, 2001, in Acra, Ghana. The violence happened when supporters of association football club Accra Hearts clashed with Oak Sporting Club's supporters. The police rushed the stadium to stop the violence, which left 127 dead, most of whom were crushed in a stampede to avoid the police.
- Montreal Canadians fans rioted in 1986, 1993, 2008, and 2010 after their team won the Stanley Cup.
- Partizan is the biggest sports club in Belgrade, Serbia and it's also one of the most organized and violent firms in Europe. The Partizan firm doesn't hold back, engaging opposing fans at basketball games and other sporting events just as much as at association football matches.
- On July 12, 1979, Chicago White Sox fans rioted at Comiskey Park in Chicago when fans were admitted for the low price of $0.98 as part of a "Disco Demolition" promotion. After a local DJ

detonated thousands of disco records brought by fans, 7,000 drunken fans rushed the field and were only stopped by the Chicago Police riot squad.

- Eastern European firms schedule what are known as "forest fights" with their rivals. The brawls are pre-arranged, far away from the watchful eyes of the police.
- FIFA tournaments held in Europe, such as the World Cup and the UEFA Championship, are sometimes marked by firm violence. English and German firms were responsible for violence at the 1998 and 2006 World Cups, and the 2000 UEFA Championship. Russian hooligans had a big impact on the 2016 UEFA Championship in France.
- Hooliganism began in ancient Rome. The Roman Emperor Marcus Aurelias (121-180 CE) wrote about the supporters of chariot racing being divided by colors: Blues, Whites, Greens, and Reds.
- The worst fan violence in South American history, and in association football history, took place on May 24, 1964, in Lima, Peru. After Peruvian fans grew violent when their team began losing to Argentina, the police moved in to quell the violence, resulting in 318 deaths.
- *The Football Factory* starring Danny Dyer is a fictional 2004 British film about hooligan firms in England.
- The Chicago Bulls won six NBA Championships in the 1990s and fan violence and rioting took place following five of those wins: 1991, 1992, 1993, 1996, and 1997.
- If you thought that tennis fans don't get violent, think again. On April 23, 1993, a crazed fan stabbed Yugoslavian tennis star Monica Seles during a match at the French Open.
- Association football hooligans are also known as "ultras" in many countries.

- The fiercest fan violence in South America is generally between supporters of the Argentine clubs Boca Juniors and River Platte. A 2007 brawl between the two groups involved knives and even guns.
- The earliest recorded fan violence, known as the Nika Riots, took place in 532 CE in Constantinople between supporters of the Blues and Greens. It's estimated 30,000 were killed.
- Fan violence has generally not been much of a problem in the NFL, but there have been several assaults and fights between opposing fans in and around stadiums in recent years. Philadelphia Eagles fans have particularly accused of being "unfriendly" to opposing fans in their stadium and rioted throughout downtown Philadelphia when the Eagles won Superbowl LII.
- Port Said, Egypt, was the scene of the worst sports violence in Middle Eastern history on February 1, 2012, when Masry hooligans went on a rampage, killing 72 Ahly fans. One Masry fan and a police officer were also killed.
- The deadliest sports violence in American history took place on June 15, 1990, in Detroit, after the Detroit Pistons won the NBA Championship. Eight people were killed, 124 injured, and 170 were arrested during the celebratory violence.

CONCLUSION

I hope you enjoyed reading *The Big Fat Book of Juicy Trivia*. Chances are, you also probably learned a few things along the way. Now that you've read this book, be sure to tell all your friends and family about it and feel free to use this information at your local pub trivia or trivia leagues.

If you're reading this conclusion, then you probably read this book cover to cover, but as I stated in the introduction, there are any number of ways you can read this book.

I'm sure that having read this book, you can see how adaptable this book can be for almost any occasion or group of friends. This book was written with the working, busy person in mind. Above all, this book was written for the sake of FUN!

Maybe some of your friends are more sports orientated, so for them, you can focus on chapter 3. Maybe you know some history buffs who will like chapter 4 or world travelers who have seen all the places mentioned in chapter 1.

Most people, of course, have friends and family who hold a diverse range of interests and backgrounds, in which case, you can focus on the potpourri of chapter 5.

Just remember, relax, kick back, and don't take things too seriously. There's plenty of time to worry about everything else in life, so when you're reading or playing *The Big Fat Book of Juicy Trivia*, it's all about fun!

DON'T FORGET YOUR FREE BOOKS

GET THEM FOR FREE ON WWW.TRIVIABILL.COM

MORE BOOKS BY BILL O'NEILL

I hope you enjoyed this book and learned something new.

Please feel free to check out some of my previous books on Amazon.

Printed in Great Britain
by Amazon